Capricorn
23 December – 20 January

First published in Great Britain 2009
by Harlequin Mills & Boon Limited,
Eton House, 18-24 Paradise Road, Richmond, Surrey TW9 1SR

Copyright © Dadhichi Toth 2008 & 2009

ISBN: 978 0 263 87071 8

Typeset at Midland Typesetters Australia

Harlequin Mills & Boon policy is to use papers that are natural, renewable and recyclable products and made from wood grown in sustainable forests. The logging and manufacturing processes conform to the legal environmental regulations of the country of origin.

Printed and bound in Spain
by Litografia Rosés S.A., Barcelona

About
Dadhichi

Dadhichi is one of Australia's foremost astrologers. He has the ability to draw from complex astrological theory to provide clear, easily understandable advice and insights for people who want to know what their future might hold.

In the 26 years that Dadhichi has been practising astrology, face reading and other esoteric studies, he has conducted over 9,500 consultations. His clients include celebrities, political and diplomatic figures, and media and corporate identities from all over the world.

Dadhichi's unique blend of astrology and face reading helps people fulfil their true potential. His extensive experience practising western astrology is complemented by his research into the theory and practice of eastern systems of astrology.

Dadhichi features in numerous newspapers and magazines and he also appears regularly on many of Australia's leading television and radio networks, where many of his political and worldwide forecasts have proved uncannily accurate.

His website www.astrology.com.au is now one of the top ten online Australian lifestyle sites and, in conjunction with www.facereader.com, www.soulconnector.com and www.psychjuice.com, they attract over half a million visitors monthly. The websites offer a wide variety of features, helpful information and personal services.

Dedicated to The Light of Intuition
Sri V. Krishnaswamy—mentor and friend
With thanks to Julie, Joram, Isaac and Janelle

Welcome from
Dadhichi

Dear Friend,

Welcome! It's great to have you here, reading your horoscope, trying to learn more about yourself and what's in store for you in 2010.

I visited Mexico a while ago and stumbled upon the Mayan prophecies for 2012, which, they say, is the year when the longstanding calendar we use in the western world supposedly stops! If taken literally, some people could indeed believe that 'the end of the world is near'. However, I see it differently.

Yes, it might seem as though the world is getting harder and harder to deal with, especially when fear enters our lives. But, I believe that 'the end' indicated by these Mayan prophecies has more to do with the end that will create new beginnings for our societies, more to do with making changes to our material view of life and some necessary adjustments for the human race to progress and prosper in future. So let's get one thing straight: you and I will both be around after 2012, reading our 2013 horoscopes!

My prediction and advice centres around keeping a cool mind and not reacting to the fear that could overtake us. Of course, this isn't easy, especially when media messages might increase our anxiety about such things as the impacts of global warming or the scarcity of fossil fuels.

I want you to understand that it is certainly important to be aware and play your part in making the world a better place; however, the best and surest way to support global goals is to help yourself first. Let me explain. If everyone focused just a little more on improving *themselves* rather than just pointing their finger to criticise others, it would result in a dramatic change and improvement; not just globally, but societally. And, of course, you mustn't forget what a positive impact this would have on your personal relationships as well.

Astrology focuses on self-awareness; your own insights into your personality, thinking processes and relationships. This is why this small book you have in your hand doesn't only concentrate on what is going to happen, but more importantly how you can *make* things happen positively through being your best.

I have always said that there are two types of people: puppets and actors. The first simply react to each outside stimulus and are therefore slaves of their environment, and even of their own minds and emotions. They are puppets in the hands of karma. The other group I call actors. Although they can't control what happens to them all the time, either, they are better able to adapt and gain something purposeful in their lives. They are in no way victims of circumstance.

I hope you will use what is said in the following pages to become the master of your destiny, and not rely on the predictions that are given as mere fate but as valuable guidelines to use intelligently when life presents you with its certain challenges.

Neither the outside world, nor the ups and downs that occur in your life, should affect your innermost spirituality and self-confidence. Take control: look beyond your current challenges and use them as the building blocks of experience to create success and fulfilment in the coming year.

I believe you have the power to become great and shine your light for all to see. I hope your 2010 horoscope book will be a helpful guide and inspiration for you.

Warm regards, and may the stars shine brightly for you in 2010!

Your Astrologer,

Dadhichi Toth

Contents

The Capricorn
Identity

*If a man's character is to be abused there's nobody like
a relative to do the business.*

—Alexander Pope

Capricorn: A Snapshot

Key Characteristics

Conventional, reserved, practical, dedicated, ambitious,
controlling, suspicious

Compatible Star Signs

Taurus, Virgo, Cancer, Scorpio and Pisces

Key Life Phrase

I acquire

Life Goals

To achieve financial security and material independence

Platinum Assets

Ambition, drive and steadiness

Zodiac Totem

The Goat

Zodiac Symbol

♍

Zodiac Facts

Tenth sign of the zodiac; cardinal, barren, feminine, dry

Element

Earth

Famous Capricorns

Kate Bosworth, Christy Turlington, Denzel Washington,
Carolyn Bessette Kennedy, J.R.R. Tolkien,
Marilyn Manson, Howard Stern, Naomi Judd, Kate Moss,
Orlando Bloom, John Singleton, LL Cool J,
Kevin Costner, Tiger Woods, Jim Carrey,
Jon Voight, Cuba Gooding Jr

Capricorn: Your profile

You have an earthy element, which in turn makes
you down-to-earth and not in the least bit an
airhead! A lack of self-confidence and self-esteem
can make you appear shy. Yours is the tenth sign
and few people are as practical and ambitious as
you. Saturn causes you to be cautious, because it
is your ruling planet.

You are not afraid of hard work and will toil
away as much as is needed to achieve your goals.
Following your dreams needs ambition, and you
have plenty of that, bringing you success in terms
of dollars. You are good at keeping track of exactly
where your money is going and prefer the tried-and-
true type of accounting for your savings. Speculation
is not on your radar.

Initially you may appear to others as slightly
cool, but there is another part of you altogether
once those same people get to know you better.
Once you are comfortable with them, you have

a side to your nature that is both humorous and affectionate. Drawing attention to yourself is not your style and you work away quietly and effectively towards your goals.

Capricorn people are generally suspicious when they meet someone for the first time. You play your cards close to your chest until a person has 'earned their stripes' with you. You want to understand just where that other person is coming from before you let down your guard.

Financial and material security is important to you and you will put in whatever hours it takes to ensure your future in this respect. You can come up with big ideas, but they will not put at risk what you have worked so hard for to achieve. Clock watching is not on your agenda and you believe in doing it right the first time so you don't have to waste time doing it again. You see this as a misuse of your time and energy.

You are not afraid of commitment and are very self-sufficient in providing yourself and loved ones with what is needed in life. You could be accused of being frugal; but again, this simply means you do not throw away hard-earned dollars on speculative deals.

You have a clear idea of where you are headed in this world and are not in the habit of asking others to help you get there. This of course means you can take full credit for your success and don't have to share the limelight with anyone else.

Capricorns are very level-headed and don't expect everything to happen in an instant. 'All good things in their own time' seems to be your motto. Your work ethics are admired by other people because they can see that you set your goal, work out your plan, and then start working on it until the end. You are very focused on where you are headed.

You prefer a traditional lifestyle and are not much interested in being 'out there', wherever 'there' happens to be. You may seem a little dull and ordinary to the more adventurous among your friends and co-workers—but so what? You are who you are. You live life on your own terms rather than compromising to suit someone else's idea of a good time. Due to this rather self-composed way of doing things, you may be seen to be looking down on others who are not living their lives as you are living yours. However, the good thing is, it doesn't really bother you what others think of your lifestyle, and you happily go about how you want to live.

Because you keep your guard up for a while until you get to know a person better, over the years you have become a great judge of character and can spot a phoney from a mile away. However, when you do get to know someone and approve of them, they will have a friend in you who is trustworthy, dependent and punctual; all in all, someone on whom they can totally rely. Any assistance you can give them will be willingly given.

You can drive a hard bargain when needs be and in money matters can be a real challenge to deal with. Sometimes you can be perceived as over materialistic.

The peaks and troughs of life are to you part of what the world is all about and you have an immense capacity to withstand whatever is thrown at you. You are resilient and can gather great strength when misfortune deals you a 'dud hand', because by dealing with it, you believe it makes you stronger.

Capricorns bring their own success by their keen focus, their discipline and single-minded concentration, and all this, combined with your ruling planet, Saturn, provides you with power and happiness in life as rewards for your long and tedious efforts.

Three classes of Capricorn

If you're a Capricorn who was born between the 23rd of December and the 1st of January, you are a true child of Saturn. You are extraordinarily determined to achieve success in life and gain a great deal of happiness through your career. Marriage and family life are also important to you but could take second place to your work.

If you were born between the 2nd and 11th of January, you are sometimes stubborn in your relationships. You can also be rather controlling and protective of your possessions and the ones you love. You are very practical and your commonsense will be one of your most distinctive assets.

If you were born between the 12th and 20th of

January your mind is concerned with perfection and doing things in the best possible way. You are attentive to the details of everything and are impeccable in your dress sense and manners. You make far-reaching plans. You are a hard taskmaster and also critical of yourself. Try focusing on the positive in your life, not only the negative.

Capricorn role model: Tiger Woods

Who hasn't heard of Tiger Woods, the famous and inspiring golfer, who, from a young age, broke so many records in the game? You wouldn't be surprised to learn that Tiger is a Capricorn and early in his life he had a dream to be the best. His tenacity, skill and ambitious determination are what helped him achieve greatness. These traits are typical of your Capricorn personality.

Capricorn: The light side

Your actions speak louder than words. Capricorns have sharp minds and, although you may be a little slower to fire up than other signs, you make fewer mistakes. Your practical mind usually gets things right the first time around, thereby saving time and effort.

Others can see you have everything under control by your calm demeanour because you don't let pressure get to you too much. This makes you a great leader and people respond to your quiet assertiveness. Perfection is high on your list of the way you do things and, although this may slow you up on the journey to your goal, it will be 100 per cent right when you get there.

Fashion is not your thing and you prefer the tried and true because your eye is on the longer-term benefits of classical clothing rather than short-lived trends. You are a graceful person and, because you are down-to-earth, your elegance and beauty may not be instantly noticeable. You are modest in exhibiting your talents and more sensible than most.

Power fascinates you and you use it justly, meting out both judgement and punishment in a reasonable manner. When in competition you play fairly. However, if someone tries to take an unfair advantage, you will clearly express your displeasure at their deceit.

Capricorn: The shadow side

You observe people and can tune in to their true character traits without them even being aware of your scrutiny. However, when the flaws in a person's character are discovered, you may use it against them as a lever, and should guard against being vindictive because you have found their weakness. Try to be as constructive as possible in your criticism of others.

Your reputation is very important to you, but it should not be a high priority in your life. Achieving wealth and influence may overshadow some of your personal relationships.

Valuable opportunities could be missed because taking risks makes you feel uncomfortable and vulnerable. Being a little tight-fisted with money does not make you open your wallet readily, but a little generosity goes a long way. 'What comes around, goes around' could be an important lesson for you to learn.

Giving can be just as much pleasure as receiving, but it may take you a little time to get used to that idea because you can be overly concerned about power and money. When you learn to share your benefits with others, your life will begin to shine.

Capricorn woman

You may at first be overlooked as not being quite as glamorous as the next woman, but your subtle beauty and grace are something many other star signs lack. You are elegant and have your own style that follows no definite trend.

Your inner character is something that not many people see until they have proven their worth to you. Because Capricorn is a deep and mystical sign, you can mistakenly be accused of chasing the almighty dollar above and beyond all else, but this is not absolutely true.

'Hardnosed' may be the way you come across to people when they first encounter you, but this is only because you are traditional in your ways and a little self-conscious in the company of others whom you don't know very well. People have to work hard to get you to open your heart and trust them because you are an amazing judge of character. Perceptive people will be attracted to your personality, which is rich and deep with subtle charisma.

Your self-motivated energy can overpower some partners because you love to compete with them. If they aren't as competent as you, they could see this as a threat. You are confident in taking on a complicated task, working hard and achieving your ambitions. You hold your head high and take on any project, standing squarely on your own two feet.

Everyone is born equal is what you believe and, with hard work and a strong focus, you achieve whatever it is you set out to do. Gender is irrelevant to you. If the best man for the job is a woman, so be it. Fierce competitiveness will be with you in the workplace, but watch that this doesn't become a serious impediment to a romantic liaison.

Life should not be taken so seriously that you forget how to laugh. Your journey through life will be much easier and more joyous if you can find a way to relax and take some well-earned time out. Venus, one of your friendly planets, indicates you have a comical and entertaining side to your personality, but perhaps others do not get to see it as often as they should. Lighten up a little.

To round out your personality, an interest in an artistic expression such as music, cultural activities or art will lead you to better friendships and increased popularity because these pursuits are also under the rulership of Venus.

Don't be rushed into making decisions and take the time you need to come to the conclusion you want. Your idea of where you are heading is clear and you know exactly how to go about achieving a particular goal. You have great strength and 110 per cent is the starting point for your efforts.

Surrounding yourself with people who can help you achieve your goals is important. Although you're capable, you also have no problem with delegating, but only to people who have proved they can do the job as well as you.

Self-centredness is a part of your personality, but this is also why you're as successful as you are. Be aware that work should not overshadow the personal side of your life because this is a danger when you are focused on a particular aim. Being a workaholic is not the path to joy and happiness.

Diplomacy is a strong point of yours. Speaking the truth without hurting the other person is a wonderful skill and with this trait you would make an outstanding judge or mediator. You mightn't say much, but when you do it has maximum impact.

Friendship is important and valued highly by you, up there with respect and reputation. Although you may not have many close friends, your loyalty to them is without equal and they are lucky people, indeed.

Capricorn man

Your air of authority almost precedes you. Saturn, the traditional and hard taskmaster, is responsible for this trait and anyone first meeting you cannot help but be made aware of your strength.

You are a born leader with your strong air of confidence, and you realise that you have this power from quite an early age. Being in control is where you like to be and is part and parcel of your Capricorn personality. You believe respect has to be earned and, throughout life, you will be respected.

Your dreams and aspirations start to form quickly and you have a sense of material success and security way before any of your peers even know what they are. Financial security is what drives you and it is part of your nature from a small child. Business, making money and anything else associated with being financially secure has a place in your mind, even in your young years.

Trifling pursuits do not interest you at all. As a result you may sometimes feel left out of the loop and a bit on the lonely side, but as you get older you'll find your niche. You'll start to enjoy life more because of your financial security and will, in fact, feel younger as you age.

You love to work and will find it hard to say no to that last-minute job or a few extra hours to get something finished. Watch that you don't become a workaholic, even though you derive an enormous amount of satisfaction from a job well done. The backlash could be a detrimental effect on your personal life, so learning to balance your life could be a challenge for you.

Although you will have only a few close friends, those you do have will be fortunate to have you as a friend. Loyal, generous and prepared to do anything for them is their luck in life; however, you do demand the same level of loyalty and generosity in return. Your cool, hardened exterior shelters a sensitive and caring human being.

You are prepared to work hard to achieve things in life and appreciate everything your efforts bring to you. Some Capricorn men have had a rather hard life as youngsters and need to work through issues of trust. If this is you, this will be your Achilles heel. Try to be less hard on yourself and remember to smell the roses along the way.

You are born with an uncanny wisdom about the world because you are an old soul. Capricorn is generally regarded as intuitive and you have the odd hunch or two that stands you in good stead. You may appear as a solitary individual but you are a private person and prefer to work on your own rather than as part of a team. Work to you is a great pleasure and you are practical and realistic.

Your main priorities as a Capricorn man are security and self-control. You are generous but your personal goals need to be fulfilled as well and unless this happens you will come across as thriftier than you need to be.

Capricorn child

Issues of power and control are evident very early in the Capricorn child. They are not easy to deal with because they want what they want, when they want it. They are mature beyond their years and come across as having an old head on young shoulders. Their inbuilt wisdom will never cease to surprise you.

They are quite clear about what they don't want, too, so give up guessing what they do want. Just ask them and they'll be more than happy to bring you up to date. They may have a quiet exterior but behind those solemn eyes is a mind that works away, being inquisitive and cooking up many plans that you may not be privy to until you need to be.

Their ambitious nature shows up early and you will find them totally focused on their schoolwork, almost to the exclusion of everything else around them. They enjoy having a good reputation and will do their work and complete assignments on time. 'Going the extra mile' is just what they like to do, but they can also be overly worried that their 110 per cent is not quite enough. Your role is to help them learn to relax while at the same time encouraging them to do their best because nothing short of perfect is okay for them.

A balance between work and play will be a lesson they must learn and carry into their adult life. Security and comfort mean a lot to a Capricorn child and are essential for them to feel happy and harmonious. A Capricorn child can get depressed because they keep all their problems to themselves and don't necessarily find it easy talking to others about private issues, which includes family members. Even when they have done exceptionally well they can still feel they have failed because they have aimed so high.

Achieving their goals is only half the job and the other half is to laugh and have fun with them. Teaching them to unwind and enjoy themselves will stand them in good stead. Fresh air and physical activity will play a big part in helping them to relieve their stress levels.

Romance, love and marriage

Capricorns often miss out on romantic opportunities right in front of them because their eyes are focused on the heavens, aiming for that grand success. This can happen time and time again because they don't see the opportunity until it is too late.

For you, Capricorn, opportunities for love and intimacy are few and far between, so when you do hear a knock on your door, for goodness' sake, open it! Don't delay by putting the finishing touches to whatever you are doing or your soulmate might just think no one is home and turn away—another opportunity lost for you.

Your life partner needs to have a high level of integrity, be hard working, and provide protection and security for you. Oh, and another thing: commitment is very important, too. This combination of qualities is not easy to find, so when they all come together in one human being, cast aside your suspicions and cynicism and get to know them. You can be a little old-fashioned when it comes to giving yourself to someone, but once you find the right person you'll completely give your body, mind and soul to them.

You will provide your life partner with some rather severe tests to prove their love to you, but don't make these tests so hard that people will inevitably fail. They must be prepared to share in the journey of life with you and accept the highs and lows; be ready, willing and able to weather the storms of life.

Not being the most demonstrative or emotional sign of the zodiac is typical of a Capricorn, but once someone has opened their heart to you and proves their love, you can be surprisingly warm and sensual in return.

Developing an underlying trust slows up the development of any of your relationships because that element is paramount to you. Your chosen partner will eventually realise that your honesty and dependability are traits that 'come with the territory' of joining their heart and soul to yours.

Your romantic ideal is very clear—just as with everything else—but sometimes your criteria are a little difficult for the average person to meet. You most hate being seen as a failure and your love life doesn't escape this, either. Just as financial success brings with it reputation, so too does your emotional success, in a similar way, prove the same.

Many female Capricorns don't readily accept the modern attitudes to love and life and prefer a conventional approach where their partners take the lead. It will take more than a few dates to sway you, and falling head over heels in love on the first date is not your style at all. You need to sift carefully through all of their character traits before you eventually tie the knot.

Romance with a Capricorn has a few quite straightforward ground rules and, if these aren't adhered to, you won't get to first base, let alone down the aisle. Laziness in a prospective suitor is enough to make a Capricorn run very fast in the opposite direction. You want your partner to work along with you, not sit back and watch your efforts.

You have a great deal of love and warmth to offer, even though your exterior may seem a little cool at first glance. Venus rules the sensual aspects of your character and shows that you do have a fire within. The relationship needs to be running smoothly before your excitement and passion come to the fore, which can happen only after the person has proved their worth. They will also need to be patient and persevering.

Your mate needs to have the same amount of on-going commitment. Your heart will be won completely if you meet someone with this quality.

The sign of Cancer rules your marriage affairs and you can, to some extent, have a great relationship with this star sign. Once your prospective partner has proven that they are right for you, this is when you will feel at ease and fully express your deepest passions.

Health, wellbeing and diet

Suppressing your feelings and bottling up emotions can have a detrimental effect on your health in general. You must, in all circumstances, talk about how you feel and, by showing your feelings, you are much less likely to suffer stress-related disorders. Bottling up your emotions causes internal tension, and if you're a sedentary type this will cause problems in your personal life.

You love to work and this can lead you to 'burning the candle at both ends'. Unfortunately you'll probably ignore your body's warning signals and just try harder to keep working. That's not a good idea at all. Working longer hours will just lead to burnout.

Because Capricorn rules the lower parts of the body, including the knees, skeletal system, tendons, skin and hair, you need to get enough exercise to keep your body in tip-top health. Exercise will keep your joints functioning freely and will deter arthritic problems later in life. Physical rigidity is associated with an inflexibility of mind; the two go hand in hand.

Yoga and other deep-breathing exercises will strengthen your knees and lungs. Quite a few Capricorns push hard at sport and injure these parts of the body. Although exercise is essential, err on the side of caution to prevent injury.

Your desire for long days of hard work could lead to vitamin deficiency due to skipping meals. This will be an issue and cause nervous irritability, so a balanced diet is essential. Vitamin B supplements can help.

If you're not eating enough natural foods such as soy bean products, then bean sprouts, egg, wheatgerm and white meats are all sources of the vitamins you need. Wholegrains and unprocessed foods are a great source of dietary nutrition for Capricorn.

To be avoided are acid-forming foods and liquids such as beer and coffee. These will aggravate an arthritic or rheumatic tendency.

To strengthen sinews and tendons, especially if you're not that young any more, take glucosamine sulphate, which will help rebuild some of that tissue. Adding some flaxseed to your diet will also improve your energy levels and is a great antioxidant.

To keep your digestive system working optimally, don't eat heavy foods or those less digestible in the evening. Your ruling planet is a slow moving one and your metabolism is slowest in the evening.

Work

Capricorn is a materialistic sign and, because you are a hard worker—which you love and comes easily to you—I would like to get you to use the energy of Venus as well. This brings out your creative potential because you don't give yourself enough credit for being expressive, imaginative and sensitive.

You're self-motivated and can run your own business if you desire to pursue an independent profession. Working for others is not something you do very well, but you can manage it if it is a stepping stone to where you really want to be. Your goal is always at the forefront of your mind.

Finance and other traditional careers are at the top of your agenda, but law, teaching, mining and other research-oriented activities are also perfect for the Capricorn temperament.

Architecture, town planning and landscape design are other avenues where you can blend your practicality and sensitivity. You may seem to be a bit of a mystery to many people because you don't show your feelings readily, but if you share your ideas and resources with colleagues, you will be repaid in many ways. These people may even help you achieve your goals quicker.

Key to karma, spirituality and emotional balance

Capricorn's catch phrase, 'I aspire', sums up the motivation for this sign of the zodiac. Wealth is certainly within your grasp, but you will have to work hard with definite goals in mind to achieve this. However, life should not be all work and no play and acquiring possessions may not bring you the love and joy you desire. A balance will bring you the peace and happiness you are looking for and this is your challenge, Capricorn.

Your lucky days

Your luckiest days are Wednesday, Friday and Saturday.

Your lucky numbers

Remember that the forecasts given later in the book will help you optimise your chances of winning. Your lucky numbers are:

8, 17, 26, 35, 44, 53

5, 14, 23, 32, 41, 50

6, 15, 24, 33, 42, 51

Your destiny years

Your most important years are 8, 17, 26, 35, 44, 53, 62, 71 and 80.

Star Sign
Compatibility

When I *eventually met* Mr Right I *had no idea that his
first name was Always.*

—Rita Rudner

Romantic compatibility

How compatible are you with your current partner,
lover or friend? Did you know that astrology can
reveal a whole new level of understanding between
people simply by looking at their star sign and that
of their partner? In this chapter I'd like to share
some special insights that will help you better
appreciate your strengths and challenges using Sun
sign compatibility.

The Sun reflects your drive, willpower and
personality. The essential qualities of two star signs
blend like two pure colours, producing an entirely
new colour. Relationships, similarly, produce their
own emotional colours when two people interact.
The following is a general guide to your romantic
prospects with others and how, by knowing the
astrological 'colour' of each other, the art of love
can help you create a masterpiece.

When reading the following I ask you to remember
that no two star signs are ever *totally* incompatible.
With effort and compromise, even the most 'difficult' astrological matches can work. Don't close
your mind to the full range of life's possibilities!
Learning about each other and ourselves is the
most important facet of astrology.

Quick-reference guide: Horoscope compatibility between signs (percentage)

	Aries	Taurus	Gemini	Cancer	Leo	Virgo	Libra	Scorpio	Sagittarius	Capricorn	Aquarius	Pisces
Aries	60	65	65	65	90	45	70	80	90	50	55	65
Taurus	70	70	70	80	70	90	75	85	50	95	80	85
Gemini	70	70	75	60	80	75	90	60	75	50	90	50
Cancer	65	80	60	75	70	75	60	95	55	45	70	90
Leo	90	70	80	70	85	75	65	75	95	45	70	75
Virgo	45	90	75	75	75	70	80	85	70	95	50	70
Libra	70	75	90	60	65	80	80	85	80	85	95	50
Scorpio	80	85	60	95	75	85	85	90	80	65	60	95
Sagittarius	90	50	75	55	95	70	80	85	85	55	60	75
Capricorn	50	95	50	45	45	95	85	65	55	85	70	85
Aquarius	55	80	90	70	70	50	95	60	60	70	80	55
Pisces	65	85	50	90	75	70	50	95	75	85	55	80

Each star sign combination is followed by the elements of those star signs and the result of their combining. For instance, Aries is a fire sign and Aquarius is an air sign and this combination produces a lot of 'hot air'. Air feeds fire and fire warms air. In fact, fire requires air. However, not all air and fire combinations work. I have included information about the different birth periods within each star sign and this will throw even more light on your prospects for a fulfilling love life with any star sign you choose.

Good luck in your search for love, and may the stars shine upon you in 2010!

Compatibility quick-reference guide

Each of the twelve star signs has a greater or lesser affinity with one another. The quick-reference guide will show you who's hot and who's not so hot as far as your relationships are concerned.

CAPRICORN + ARIES

Earth + Fire = Lava

Taking a dog for a walk is not much fun if it keeps lunging forward, yanking at the lead, while you're trying to take a relaxed, leisurely stroll. You know what I'm talking about, Capricorn, especially if you happen to be hitched to an Aries!

Just like that frantic, energetic puppy, Aries is always on the go and may be prone to pulling you here, there and everywhere against your will. You see, Capricorn, the sign you were born under is much more steady, traditional and less prone to such frenzied and spontaneous activity. And this is a major obstacle for a match between you and Aries.

You're born under the element of earth, while Aries is a fire sign. This elemental mixture is not exactly a great combination. In your case, your ruling planets, Saturn and Mars respectively, are also quite antagonistic to each other.

Being practical and ambitious, with very powerful, traditional flavours to your character, Aries finds you much like a master with a leash, always trying to contain and thwart their spontaneity and zest for life. This is not really the case; it's only their perception of you. But if you both choose to enter into a relationship, a huge amount of compromise is going to be necessary to make it work. You are just so very different in your attitudes, and one of you is going to have to concede.

Not just romantically, but sexually as well, the Capricorn–Aries match is a challenge for you. Aries likes to be demonstrative and speak about their emotions and feelings, whereas Capricorn is much more likely to hold back in showing affection, at least until they feel confident that they can trust their Aries partner. Will this be quick enough for Aries, is the question. Well, to you, that's not the issue. It's whether or not they're prepared to be patient enough for you to warm to them.

As long as you give Aries enough scope for them to exercise their love of freedom, and they in turn are prepared to allow you the timely pace that you require to achieve your ends, this may give your relationship a possibility for survival. Overall, however, this is a better professional or social combination than a romantic one. If you choose to enter into business together there's every likelihood you'll be successful.

In a relationship with Aries born between the 21st and the 31st of March, there could be a clash of temperaments, with these individuals being very impulsive, reactive and hot-headed. This doesn't at all suit your down-to-earth personality.

With Aries born between the 1st and the 10th of April, you could expect a considerable amount of frustration on both sides of the fence. These characters have strong egos and won't listen all that much to your advice, even if they know what you're saying is true.

Those Aries born between the 11th and the 20th of April are big characters who have far-sighted plans, much like yourself. You will appreciate the fact that they are ambitious and industrious but are not quite as patient as you in achieving these ends.

CAPRICORN + TAURUS
Earth + Earth = Solid Ground

Taurus are some of the most steady, down-to-earth and practical people you could hope to meet. You quietly admire their resilience and their determination and also love the fact that they are very attuned to your material objectives in life.

The main reason that a Capricorn–Taurus relationship is likely to work quite well is that you are both born under the same earth element of the zodiac. When the elements are in tune, the general make-up of the people involved in the relationship is also likely to be compatible. You see a lot of yourself in each other.

Unlike Aries, the fiery, impulsive, faster-than-a-speeding-bullet character, you'll enjoy the steadier, more relaxed pace that dependable Taurus will offer you. They're very supportive, and not just on emotional and mental levels, but on practical and professional levels, too. The two of you can work together to achieve some wonderful results as a couple.

Taurus, although an earth sign, is much more sensual and demonstrative in sharing their feelings. But they are not that much interested in hurrying a relationship and so, therefore, you'll appreciate every aspect of the way they respond to you. This will draw you into their sensual and sexual atmosphere, providing you with a safe, secure base from which to begin to open your heart to them. Your thoughts and feelings work in a two-way exchange, which is comfortable for both of you.

You are a moveable or changeable sign, but Taurus is fixed and therefore much more unyielding in their opinions. You may need to adjust yourself to accept the fact they are not amenable to change as much as you are. Taurus does tend to grasp things, to hold onto the past, and also to dig in their heels. Changing their opinions is not an easy task and you'll probably learn this sooner rather than later.

You need to be a little more expressive with Taurus, who loves to explore the sensual aspects of life, not just in respect of sex, but in terms of food and other creature comforts. By speaking about what you want, they'll be more than happy to oblige you and fulfil you in every possible way. Your Taurus counterpart is demonstrative and affectionate and they like to see you enjoy this part of them to the max.

There's a particularly strong feeling of attraction between yourself and those Taureans born between the 21st and the 29th of April. Venus is a powerful ruler of these individuals, making them sensual, affectionate and very caring. You'll feel good in their company, and you'll be more likely to let down your guard and express yourself with them.

The group of Taureans born between the 30th of April and the 10th of May are not quite as compatible with you but they can still give you lots of fun and make great friends. They have an unusual sense of humour so you'll find yourself being drawn to them again and again.

Overall Taurus is a great sign for you to team up with, but you're more than likely most compatible with those who are born between the 11th and the 21st of May, because they are also ruled by Saturn, the planet ruling Capricorn. This is like meeting a soulmate and your financial and material lives will be particularly highlighted in this wonderful relationship together.

CAPRICORN + GEMINI
Earth + Air = Dust

Don't dismiss Geminis too quickly, until you get a chance to taste the extraordinary variety and versatility they offer you, especially mentally. These individuals are excellent communicators and, although you may not be one of the most outspoken zodiac signs, you still appreciate clever communication and are fascinated by the abilities of anyone you come across who has these intellectual skills.

This is where a little patience will draw you closer to Gemini, even though in the astrological scheme of things you're not particularly well suited to them. They have a very diverse and exciting way of looking at the world around them and you may seem a little stodgy to them; stifling their character somewhat.

With Gemini, you must give them free rein to express everything that is bubbling forth out of their inquisitive minds. If you start to tell them how to live their lives, the relationship will soon be over. Your element of earth and their ruling element of air don't particularly blend well and result in dust. In the extreme cases I've seen with this combination, a dust storm makes it hard to see anything.

With time, and with a Gemini who is open to learning and evolving, you'd be the ideal partner for teaching them how to ground themselves and focus on achieving lifelong goals. In this way you can act as an anchoring mentor for their scattered ways.

Capricorn and Gemini are a complex combination and, although a Gemini would hate to admit it, you can teach them some valuable lessons in managing not just the financial elements of material life but the day-to-day routines and ways of living most efficiently.

You have a great interest in money and financial security and, while Gemini loves to partake of all this if it's offered, it's best to let them operate on a creative, communicative level and for you to take full control of the dollars and the cents. If you both agree, you will have one less problem to deal with as a couple.

Gemini is ruled by Mercury, a youthful and playful planet, whereas Saturn, your ruler, is seen as a solitary planet, a hermit. Because of this, the compatibility rating for both of you, especially in the bedroom, is not all that great. Try to remain a little more open to Gemini's humour and role-playing and you might just learn something about what true sexual pleasure is about.

Your relationship with Geminis born between the 22nd of May and the 1st of June will not be an easy one. These Geminis don't have any particular rhyme or reason to the way they live life, and this could drive you batty. You will need to exercise some control over them for this to work.

If you're in a relationship with a Gemini born between the 2nd and the 12th of June, consider yourself lucky. Although I've said that a relationship with Gemini is not the best, you do feel a natural attraction for each other and this is one combination that may just work, even though you'll feel quite strung out by their effervescent lifestyles.

Geminis born between the 13th and the 21st of June are particularly communicative and love intellectual pursuits. As long as you can keep up with the constant discussions and have something to contribute intellectually, the relationship should be reasonably good.

CAPRICORN + CANCER
Earth + Water = Mud

You probably need a personality like Cancer to soften you, Capricorn. You need more sensitivity, a connection to your heart level and the softer side of life, and Cancer will most certainly be able to do that for you.

Being ruled by the Moon and also your opposite zodiac sign, there is an opportunity that awaits you with a Cancerian partner. But don't let confusion rule this relationship. You need to be clear and continue to be grounded because Cancer, being

44

extremely changeable and moody, could get the better of you from time to time.

Although Cancer is very demonstrative and caring, being ruled by the Moon means that their personalities are rather volatile and unpredictable. The emotional aspect of your relationship could become exasperating if you get too entangled in their changeable moods.

If you're happy to let your Cancer partner dominate the domestic environment while you 'bring home the bacon', then this relationship will have clearly defined roles that allow you to operate at your best in your own individual environments, combining your talents to make for a happy life together.

Cancer has an intuitive, emotional response to life and you are much more practical and factual in the way you approach things. Respect each other on these points because these very different attitudes are not necessarily mutually exclusive and it's likely, being opposites, that you will attract and can make the relationship work.

You like being supported and nurtured by Cancer and they enjoy the fact that, in return, you offer them the financial and material security they also greatly need. Just remember, however, that money for Cancer is only a means to an end and should never be placed above human relationships in an order of priority.

Sexually and intimately speaking, you need to 'step up to the plate' to demonstrate your feelings and show that you do have a heart. Otherwise, Cancer will be greatly disappointed and wounded in a spiritual sense. You may not mean to do this but they are particularly sensitive and need to know that you love them. This could be hard for you because you like to show your love in much more tangible ways and not necessarily emotionally. Explain the situation to them; keep the lines of communication open and over time you may just strike a happy balance together.

Getting together with a Cancer born between the 22nd of June and the 3rd of July will warm your heart and make you much more sensitive as a human being. This is a reasonably good match and if you're looking for a secure marriage partner with a Cancerian, this group is certainly one that may work.

Your relationship with Cancerians who are born between the 4th and the 13th of July will be one of great friendship and mutual support. However, they are quite emotional and can be volatile and reactive if they don't get their own way. Cancers born between the 14th and the 23rd of July are attracted to you but you may feel a friendship is better with them than a romantic association. There's a strong spiritual and karmic connection between the two of you.

CAPRICORN + LEO
Earth + Fire = Lava

Leo might never even know you feel uncomfortable by the fact that they continually outshine you. This doesn't mean they're better than you, just that they're always busy parading their abilities, their achievements and their personalities to the world at large.

You too have great skills, talents and abilities, but are not as likely to want to showcase these in public and, therefore, in your relationship with Leo, you may continually take a backseat. How long can you play second-fiddle to your partner? You'll either need to assert yourself and change your ways, or simply endure or perhaps even enjoy the spectacle of your life with a Leo partner.

By enjoying your life with them, I mean that you could expect an incredible upswing in your social agenda. Leos love to be with other people and, if this is not your cup of tea, then forget it! You're best to find someone a little more low-key and less showy if a quiet, hermitic life is what you prefer.

Leo is often traditional, like yourself, even if they do tend to be show-offs. Leo loves to try new things, to innovate and at times shock others, whereas you would rather do things in a more measured way, with a traditional approach. Remember, Leo is ruled by the element of fire, and you have that earthiness about you.

It will never be a dull moment with Leo, who is brash, improvisational and always entertaining. They are larger-than-life characters and, as soon as you let go of your self-image—your preconditioning—you'll start to relax and more than likely enjoy your time with them.

You are linked to each other through the mechanism of money and sex. There's a strong karmic link in this respect, and for some reason or other, you'll both be dealing with these issues as a means of leveraging power. You must never try to dominate each other in this relationship, because you are both strong characters. Sharing power is a better way to look at a successful arrangement between a Capricorn and Leo.

There are three categories of Leos and those born between the 5th and the 14th of August will not seem as abrasive to you as some of the others. They have a wonderfully optimistic and appreciative nature and you also love the fact they are generous to a fault.

Try to give Leos born between the 24th of July and the 4th of August some latitude in their behaviour, even if you don't initially approve of them. They have a very powerful solar influence, which means they need to show their talents to the world. Clipping their wings would be a great mistake and would quickly end your relationship with them.

Leos born between the 14th and the 23rd of August are not at all a good match for you. They are, like yourself, highly motivated, but hate being controlled, as do you. They may try to take charge, and this would mean either biting your tongue, or exiting stage left.

CAPRICORN + VIRGO
Earth + Earth = Solid Ground

Flexibility is an important part of making a relationship work with Virgo. Even though you are both born under the same element of earth, which is an excellent basis for your relationship, Virgo is a rather difficult match in that they have a very keen eye for detail and often turn that magnifying glass of scrutiny onto other people, their personalities, and the relationship as a whole.

Virgo is analytical to a fault. When it comes to questioning you on the whys and wherefores of your life, you could be made to feel rather uncomfortable. On the one hand you'll appreciate their intellectual and communicative manner, but their obsession with detail could start to bother you. Actually, Capricorn also has a need to understand the detail but there's usually a very good reason for it. You see, Virgo's love of detail is almost an obsession; detail for the sake of detail and only always detail. This will drive you nuts.

On a positive note, Virgo is a youthful sign, being ruled by Mercury, and if you've been bogged down in work and other traditional day-to-day activities that haven't given you much scope to enjoy life, Virgo will help you rediscover the child within once again.

Once you get to know them, Virgos have a great sense of humour and they're constantly seeking out new and pleasurable pursuits and intellectual interests. By teaming up with them, you'll be enjoying new paths that will open up many exciting vistas of experience to you.

You'll make a strong impact in the life of Virgo and this relationship is likely to be a two-way street where you can easily share your love and your affection for each other. As I said earlier, Virgo needs to tone down their critical side if you are to feel comfortable with opening up further to them. Working together is also an excellent idea because both of you are methodical and attentive to your work and can fit into each other's daily routine quite easily. This could be a good work as well as love relationship.

There are Virgos who are born between the 24th of August and the 2nd of September and these individuals are quite spiritually orientated. You can take their advice and use them as mentors because what they have to say will aid your emotional development. There's some teaching, legal or counselling aptitude with them, and you may even meet through these activities.

Virgos born between the 3rd and 12th of September are an excellent match for any Capricorn. You have much in common because Saturn also co-rules them. Your destiny seems to fit well with theirs and financial success could also be part of the bigger picture for the two of you.

With Virgos born between the 13th and the 23rd of September, your attraction towards each other is quite compelling. These individuals have the added influence of Venus, making them lovers of pleasure and very amorous as well. This is a bonus in your relationship.

CAPRICORN + LIBRA
Earth + Air = Dust

If you think that Libra will drop everything to dedicate their life wholly and solely to you, focusing on no one else but you, you're very much mistaken. You must cast aside any possessiveness if you are going to embark on a relationship with Libra.

You see, Libra, ruled by the sociable and loving Venus, won't stand for any sort of jealous envy of their friendships outside your relationship. This is who they are. They are wired for love, social interaction and variety, which they believe is the spice of life.

As a Capricorn, you're quite decisive and determined in your choices when life throws up a situation that requires action. You perceive in Libra an inability to make up their mind and, yes, they are rather changeable as far as the star signs are concerned. They oscillate and require a lot of input before coming to a conclusion. You can forgive this aspect to some extent, but if you see it as an ingrained personality trait, you may start to lose respect. And once that goes, what's left in a relationship, I ask?

The problem you'll have, even if Libra doesn't live up to your expectations, is that they have such a loving nature and, once they pamper you with just a fraction of their sensuous and affectionate energy, you'll be hooked—or rather, should I say—addicted to them. It won't be easy letting go of this warmth and sensitivity that they possess and shower upon you.

Perhaps your lesson with Libra is to let go of your envy, let go of the idea that a relationship is something you own. By relaxing these precon-ditioned ideas, you'll be better poised to enjoy a relationship. And this, taken a step further, will give you the most magnificent experience sexually, not just emotionally.

Openness is the secret to a good match between a Capricorn and a Libran. Generally speaking, Libra possesses many traits that run against the grain of your own personality, making it a challenging relationship for you, to say the least.

Librans born between the 24th of September and the 3rd of October are particularly affectionate and social creatures and can easily win over your heart.

Those Librans born between the 4th and the 13th of October are rather unusual personalities. They're quite unpredictable in many ways. This can really set alarm bells off in your opinion and you may be rather reluctant to 'dive into the deep end' with them, so to speak. Maintaining an open mind will be the key to proceeding with these people.

Librans born between the 14th and the 23rd of October have much to do with your personal and spiritual development and will appear in your life when you least expect it. They have a youthful personality and can soften that serious Saturnine element of your character to make you a much more trusting and loving individual. It seems that at least this group of Librans may be of great benefit to your life.

CAPRICORN + SCORPIO
Earth + Water = Mud

Some star signs, when trying to deal with Scorpio, use all sorts of mental strategies and techniques to understand and dominate them. Therefore, at the outset, I'd like to warn you that this ploy just won't work with them, so don't even go there!

You're a strong character, like your Scorpio counterpart, but you need to be transparent and not play mind games with them. You have to understand Scorpio is the master of mental challenges, so even if you attempt it, you're unlikely to win.

Your ruling planets—Saturn and Mars respectively—are not particularly friendly, and so astrologically speaking this is not a great match. However, in some instances, having an initial friendship as the basis of your relationship can make it blossom into something worthwhile and lasting.

Remaining aloof, cool and detached is not the way to win the heart of a Scorpio. This could be a stumbling block for you. Unless you're prepared to 'shape up', then 'ship out' because you need to warm to Scorpio and express yourself, not in a reserved but a passionate manner. You'll quickly see just how passionate and dynamic the Scorpio personality is, and they demand nothing less than an equal if you want them to love you.

The sexual compatibility of a Capricorn and a Scorpio is complicated. In some ways your detached attitude entices Scorpio even more because they see this as a call to a challenge. Scorpios love challenges, and therefore, as long as you're prepared to reciprocate sexually, physically and lustfully, Scorpio will feel that the challenge was well worth it.

With Scorpios born between the 24th of October and the 2nd of November, a great friendship is likely to arise, but don't be surprised that this relationship gradually develops into something richer and more enduring.

Scorpios born between the 3rd and the 12th of November have a touch of Pisces in them and are therefore spiritual and compassionate individuals. Their intuitive powers are strong and so they'll see through any of your mental tricks. They also expect you to be generous with your money and, as you know, Capricorn is primarily concerned with money and financial security. Just be prepared to share a bit of it around if you want to keep these Scorpios in your life.

You'll be challenged by Scorpios born between the 13th and the 22nd of November. Passionate, intense and demanding on every level, you'll still find their magnetic charm irresistible. Because of this it's quite likely a Capricorn and a Scorpio born in this time frame are possibly even suited to marriage.

CAPRICORN + SAGITTARIUS
Fire + Earth = Lava

You can deny it all you like, but deep down you'll know it's true when I tell you that secretly you wish you could be as carefree, adventurous and optimistic as Sagittarius is. Perhaps this is why you are attracted to them. You have a reserved and less-than-positive attitude in life, and associating with Sagittarius at least gives you a taste for what it would be like to be completely free of your self-limiting concepts.

Your detached and inward-looking character is activated by the outward-bound, larger than life, uninhibited and generous Sagittarius. With this character, you'll absolutely enjoy life so much more. But you'll never fully be able to let go of yourself, because concern for the future and your material wealth is a genetic coding you just will never be able to shake off. Just allow yourself those moments of freedom to balance your inbuilt Capricorn personality. In doing so, Sagittarius will at least feel you're making an effort to explore their way of life.

Sagittarius is open to your suggestions of being more practical, living life with a greater degree of planning and efficiency. But they'll never fully give up their love of independence and freedom, so you need to get used to that idea. The two of you will need to find that happy balance, a harmonious blend of financial life and security with travel, social interaction and life exploration.

Sagittarius, being ruled by the fire element, is able to warm you, elevate you and bring you to a new level of shared understanding. This relationship can be a stimulating one if you're the type of Capricorn who is open to what life has to offer.

Sexually, your chemistry with Sagittarius isn't quite as hot as they would like it to be. Let's face it: you can't pretend to be hotter than you are, can you? But once again, keeping an open heart and mind and inviting Sagittarius to share their ways with you, will make them a little more patient and understanding.

A great meeting of the minds can be expected with Sagittarians born between the 23rd of November and the 1st of December, in that they are less fiery than the typical Sagittarian, and quite compatible with your own sign. Spend time together and investigate each other's personality. Do you like what you find, and vice versa?

For Sagittarians born between the 2nd and the 11th of December, the relationship may not go all that smoothly. You both have very set ideas about how you want to live your lives and therefore a confrontation of egos is quite likely. This is not a particularly great match.

Your relationship with Sagittarians born between the 12th and the 22nd of December is also quite trying. You need to move slowly—that is, if they can, too—to establish just how compatible you are together. There might be a sense that you are not cut out to spend too much time with each other.

CAPRICORN + CAPRICORN
Earth + Earth = Solid Ground

As long as you and your star twin, Capricorn, vow at the outset to work at stimulating each other in this relationship, you may well find out you are extremely well suited.

Being with another Capricorn is a consolation in that they understand where you are coming from and you, too, have a sense of what they wish to prioritise in life. Because of this you are most able to support each other, making a mutually beneficial relationship that offers a solid, steady and loving outcome.

As a Capricorn, you know how important it is for you to have a stable financial and material life, and being with a Capricorn will help make this dream a reality. You are both purposeful in your action, and will pool your resources together quite nicely to create a wonderful lifestyle for yourselves and a family if you choose to have one.

It's interesting how Capricorns are so ambitious and capable of achieving their goals, yet at the same time, in my own experience, I have found them to be rather depressed. Don't let any despondency or melancholia undermine your relationship. At least, with some of the other star signs such as Sagittarius or Leo, you have a counteractive warmth and brightness that may not be found with another Capricorn. Try to lift yourselves out of your own personal dark moods, and this should augur well for the two of you.

You'd probably prefer to forfeit the sexual excitement of some of the other signs for the security and comfort you find with another Capricorn. At least you know where you stand with them and there won't be too many surprises. The only problem with this match is that you may both become a little too despondent as time goes by. Try to be a little more creative together in this department.

Generally most Capricorns get on with each other, but with those born between the 23rd of December and the 1st of January, the additional influence of Venus makes for a higher degree of affection between you. This can't but help make you both feel happier.

Those born between the 2nd and the 10th of January are the most amorous among the Capricorn-born individuals. Therefore a natural affinity between those born between the 23rd of December and the 1st of January and those born between the 2nd and the 10th of January is quite evident.

Those of you born in different periods also have a reasonably good chance of surviving in a serious relationship, especially with other Capricorns born between the 11th and 20th of January.

CAPRICORN + AQUARIUS
Earth + Air = Dust

What can I say? The two of you are diametrically opposed! Aquarius is the revolutionary star sign of the zodiac, whereas you, Capricorn, are quite traditional, preferring the tried and tested values of conservative life. There are many dissimilarities between you, which are obvious at the outset, starting with your respective ruling planets Saturn and Uranus being at odds with each other.

You'll find Aquarius is experimental and progressive in every facet of their lives. You've got no problem respecting this in someone else until they start to try to impose it upon you. You need to get with the times, or change your ways and think in a more modern fashion, is what your Aquarian partner may start to throw at you. This will make you feel uncomfortable because, when change happens for Capricorn, it is usually at a much slower pace than Aquarius prefers.

'The age of Aquarius' has to do with breaking down, morphing and transforming everything traditional. This is not easy for you, Capricorn, because you like to build things up slowly, solidly and usually with a view to permanency. This is where a relationship between Capricorn and Aquarius is so full of tension. Can these opposites work?

Sex with an Aquarian is exploratory. You need to take your mind into a whole new realm of insight if you're to meet them on their terms. Aquarius wants to take lovemaking to a whole new level. An old-fashioned approach is not to their liking, which could see you at odds with each other. You're more than happy to try new things but Aquarius needs to understand that a gentle nudge works far better with you than a bomb under the bed.

In your relationship with an Aquarian born between the 21st and the 30th of January, you'll soon realise that they are the revolutionaries of the zodiac and you don't feel at all comfortable with the way they wish to bulldoze through things. They need to go at a slower, steadier pace if they are to satisfy you and make this relationship work.

There are some Aquarians who are light-hearted and quite funny, too, and they tend to be born between the 31st of January and the 8th of February. They can bring a smile to your face, Capricorn, but it's still rather dubious as to whether or not a long-term relationship with them is likely.

You feel reasonably comfortable intellectually and sensually with those Aquarians born between the 9th and the 19th of February. Venus brings to them great taste and an affectionate nature. You are quite a frugal personality whereas they are excessive by nature. On this count you are quite different.

CAPRICORN + PISCES
Earth + Water= Mud

Once you get your head around the idea that Pisces lives in a completely different world to you, this relationship can be quite a formidable one. 'A different world?' you ask. Well, I say that figuratively. Pisces is concerned with the subtler forces of nature, of intuitive responses to life and a spiritual connectedness to all things. Does this sound a little too airy-fairy? Perhaps.

But Pisces does tend to offer you great mateship and a balance to your practical and sometimes serious attitude. And you similarly are a great balance for them, being able to bring them down to earth, and utilise their unique insights for the good of others in the most practical manner.

Pisces live life with their hearts, not their heads. They're the dreamers of the zodiac, being ruled by the subtle and spiritual Neptune. You must never demean them for having their dreams because they are able to act as a fuel for the more practical people among us such as yourself, Capricorn. You operate from the head level and have a great capacity for sustained work and self-sacrifice. Therefore the two of you can act as wonderful counterbalances to each other if your hearts and minds unite with a common goal.

You mustn't become too wrapped up in your work, because Pisces needs their attention towards you reciprocated. It mightn't seem like it, because they are rather selfless people. But never forget that they're human, just like you. Take the time to give them the affection they require from their partner. Pisces will try to satisfy each and every one of your needs, especially sexually. They're sensitive, caring and they're also very intuitive as to what you need at any given moment. You'll be fully satisfied by their loving ways.

Pisces born between the 20th and the 28th or 29th of February are the idealistic individuals. You could find it difficult to relate to them because they appear to be completely unconcerned with practical life. This could undermine your confidence in the relationship but I suggest you delve a little deeper to see whether or not there's something worth retrieving in a relationship with them. It may just work.

Those Pisces born between the 1st and the 10th of March are powerfully influenced by the Moon and Cancer, and so they're rather moody, sensitive types. Notwithstanding this, you do have a mutual attraction for each other that can make you feel loved and supported. This is therefore a reasonably good match.

You could become great friends and lovers with Pisces born between the 11th and the 20th of March. However, never rule the household with an iron fist if you're involved with these Pisceans. Show them affection, love and understanding and this will improve your relationship and even your sexual satisfaction together.

2010:
The Year Ahead

> *The secret to success is to own nothing, but control*
> *everything.*
>
> —Nelson Rockefeller

Romance and friendship

The year 2010 is a particularly important year for all Capricorns. Romance, love and emotional ties will be spotlighted, especially in the very first few days of 2010. First and foremost, your ruling planet Saturn occupies the upper part of the horoscope in its most dignified sign of Libra. This gives you a sense of power, of seeking those things in life you believe you deserve, which will make you happy throughout the coming twelve months and beyond.

Secondly, a powerful lunar eclipse on the first of the month, on the first day of the year, strongly points to some very important decisions being made in love and marriage.

The planet of love, Venus, is in close proximity to the influence of this eclipse, which is well-known astrologically to bring up important emotional issues from your past. These issues will most certainly impact on the current status of your relationships, whether you're single or married.

This is a significant time because if you've felt short changed in your relationships, you'll be making every effort, and intensely so, to demand what you feel you deserve. Some Capricorns, due to the difficult aspect between Venus and Saturn, will feel as though they deserve to be treated better, to be acknowledged for their contribution in their relationships and, if this is you, you'll finally realise your own worthiness and take every step towards fulfilling these inner needs.

To further intensify these astrological indicators, a solar eclipse on the 15th is preceded by your ruling planet moving retrograde on the 13th. These two celestial events also point to very strong changes being likely in your closest relationships. There are serious ramifications, but if you handle your romantic issues with grace, dignity and honesty, you'll make some important breakthroughs. These breakthroughs will act as a great foundation for improved relationships in the future, not just romantically, but socially as well. These celestial signals reflect changes in any and all of your most important relationships this year.

In February, Venus, the love planet that influences your romantic affairs, comes in close contact with Neptune, the planet of spirituality and idealism, around the 8th. Your vision for a better relationship, for true love, will come into focus and, as long as you maintain your practicality, you'll be able to balance your vision of love with what's possible in this worldly realm. You may have to make some sacrifices at this time but it will be well worth it, especially if you truly love the person whom you're with.

Opportunities abound at this time, due to Venus and Jupiter giving you the 'gift of the gab'. Words will flow from your mouth easily and vice versa;

others will speak kindly and generously to and of you. Your reputation will grow and you will have the opportunity to attract a better calibre of person into your social sphere.

In March and April there are some exciting trends forecast for you as Venus contacts Uranus and also influences your domestic sphere. This indicates a desire to break free of your traditional limitations and boldly go for experiences you may not have tried before, irrespective of your age.

A new love affair or romantic interest is quite likely when Venus transits your zone of love affairs after the 1st of April. With Saturn also moving through your zone of values, ethics and religion around the 8th, your whole view of life will be shaken to its core. Your nearest and dearest may not understand the change of heart and way you are approaching discussions, social gatherings and life generally.

Marriage, commitment and long-term ties are the themes for you when Venus enters your zone of marriage around the 20th of May. Some of you who historically have been tethered to your family will decide to fly the coop when Uranus also makes its impact felt on your domestic sphere in the latter part of May. Any indecision you've had in your inner circle, with family members or loved ones, will be greatly clarified in the very last few days of May. It's full steam ahead with a whole new life plan at this time. Wow.

A fortunate turn of events is forecast for you in

June when Jupiter and Mars influence your decisions and your actions. It's time to create a better life for yourself on the home front. You'll 'step up to the plate' and speak your mind without fear of antagonising anyone. If flatmates, partners or spouses have been on your case, constraining you in any way, you can break free and assert your independence during this cycle.

These influences are also again powerfully highlighted on the 26th of June in your Sun sign. This can have a marked impact on your emotions, based upon your early home life and upbringing. If you've been harbouring old hurts, grievances or perhaps grudges with some of your closest family members, it's time for an inner spring cleaning. This will clear the air and give you the confidence to enjoy life and love once again on your own terms.

Friendships could hit a snag throughout July, which could be the result of a difference of opinion between you and one or more people in your peer group. This is another reason for obvious changes in your relationships as Venus transits your zone of long-distance journeys. Someone you're close to may leave the scene, or you yourself may choose to travel and exit your usual day-to-day activities.

For some born under Capricorn, the powerful transit of your ruling planet in the career sector means you may not even have time to spend with those whom you love and enjoy being with. Additional responsibilities will weigh heavily on you. Divided loyalties may be the cause of a rift between you and your stable friends. Sometimes decisions at different times in your life require you to step back and do what has to be done, even if others don't accept your decisions at the time. Stand by your choices because life has bigger and better things in store for you, even if it doesn't seem that way right now.

In August, Mars and Saturn will be very devitalising. Look after your health and try not to please too many people at once. You get some temporary relief from the stresses and strains of modern day life by the entry of Venus into your zone of career at this time. This will bring you more social satisfaction, which helps you to forget the problems of the previous month or two. These influences continue throughout August and September.

Familiarity breeds contempt after the 15th when Mars makes its presence felt in your zone of friendships, so try to speak a little less and not get too bogged down in differences of opinion, especially philosophical or political opinions. You could be in for a few squabbles, and for the sake of a few idealistic differences, it would be a shame to lose a good long-term friend. I suggest you bite your tongue for a little while.

A loved one may have a change of heart in October. Something they told you and you trusted may not come to fruition. They may make all sorts of excuses for why they've had to make such a dramatic about-face and, if you get bogged down in the hows and wherefores, you may also have to say 'goodbye'. But it needn't be this way.

November is a low-key period where you should trust your inner promptings to take some time out and be with yourself. Mars enters your zone of secrets and spiritual activity. Get away from the hustle and bustle of daily life and do this alone. Recharge your inner batteries to give yourself the energies required to complete the year with a clear mind and healthy body.

The year finishes on a rather unusual note with a lunar eclipse in your zone of service and work. You may have been offered some sort of assistance in the past, and at this time you may be called upon to repay the debt. This is a karmic issue. It will give you the opportunity to help someone become better and, in turn, this will help you. If you approach this request for help with a spiritual attitude, it will bring you that much closer to the person in question.

The year 2010 should be one in which many new doors open for you romantically and a period where your spiritual growth is also very much assured.

Work and money

You can truly make your mark professionally throughout 2010, and the reason for this is the huge strength of your ruling planet Saturn throughout the coming two years. For the first time in nearly 30 years, Saturn will reach its greatest point of dignity in the zodiac, which can mean only good things for you in terms of your career, material aspirations and financial fulfilment.

No doubt you will feel a considerable weight on your shoulders, but because these responsibilities are making you better at what you do, you'll welcome any career challenge with open arms. In January you will capture the attention of your superiors through your dedication and excellent work practices. You may not gain the full measure of what you would like to receive as a financial reward, but Jupiter transiting your income zone will see to it that you'll have sufficient to make whatever you do worth your while this year.

In February and March, you may want to speculate, take some risks in your work and venture into new and uncharted territories. This would be a good thing for you, especially if you've been anchored to the same job for far too long. In March, when Venus and Uranus influence your zone of travel, communications and daily affairs, your mind will be switched on and ready to make a big break. Have no fear, because your courage will carry you forward and give you many opportunities you hadn't even dreamed of previously.

You can make great inroads into your commercial and business partnerships throughout May and June. Venus offers you an excellent rapport with existing or potentially new business partners throughout May, especially the latter part. If you're looking for seed funding for a project, some new creative idea that requires financial backing, you have the charm and persuasiveness to state your case and gain all the support you need at this time.

In July excellent opportunities arise for investment in property and fixed assets. Being an earth sign, you're always very mindful of not wasting your money and being practical in every aspect of your financial dealings. This idea extends to things in which you wish to invest. You're not one for get-rich-quick schemes, and therefore investing in land, property and other traditional assets would be a good idea during this phase of the year. You'll gain considerably through solid, steady, albeit slow, investments.

You need to have the courage of your convictions during 2010! It would be easy for you to stay in the same old groove and not step out into the limelight, into new and exciting pathways that will lead you to bigger and better things. Fearlessness, initiative and a positive, up-beat approach is what will win you success in the coming twelve months.

Don't let frustrations build up too strongly in July. There may be financial plans you have in place that need to be put on the backburner for a while. The Sun will move through the zone of your horoscope relating to shared finances, banks, taxes and other financial issues that could be in the hands of others. With Mars and Saturn combining in your career sector, expect delays, confusion and generally things to proceed much slower than you would prefer. Patience will pay off handsomely.

August is an excellent period in which you can mix your social and business activities to gain an unfair advantage over others. Venus endows you with considerable charm and makes life much easier for you. You'll find yourself winning the race in several directions and without too much effort on your part, I might add.

Profits should be up when Venus moves through your eleventh zone of increased social activity and business profitability. Coupled with Jupiter moving through your zone of contracts around the 9th of September, this is a double-whammy for success all round!

However, sudden changes in contracts and communications around the 19th may cause you to doubt yourself or perhaps to doubt the support of others. You must continue to stand on your own two feet rather than rely on others to carry you across the finishing line. The key words throughout this year do seem to be 'independence' and 'self-initiative'.

You're particularly creative around October. Don't hold back at presenting your ideas, even if they seem a little far-fetched. Someone may feel inspired by what you have to say and, even though you may not be able to get the concept into full swing immediately, it is something that will slowly grow over time and definitely bring you some financial benefits at the end of the line. So persist with the idea, even in the face of criticism on the home front.

Your physical drive and vitality is increased as Mars enters your Sun sign around the 8th of December. You could expect the last month of 2010 to be hectic, exciting and again profitable. The lunar eclipse in your sixth zone of work on the 21st, just before Christmas, indicates last-minute changes and a need to adjust yourself hastily to capitalise on the prevailing trends.

Karma, luck and meditation

Luck is more a matter of initiative and self-application than some sort of accidental event. If you are to believe in the doctrine of karma, then what happens to you is simply a result of previous actions, even if you don't necessarily recollect them. This is your time, Capricorn, and, with your ruling planet moving through its most powerful zone in 30 years, you will experience an upswing in luck, vitality, honour and respect from everyone around you.

This is a year when your successes will be marked by your diligence and self-application, although you may find yourself burdened with extra responsibilities. But this won't worry you because somehow, innately you understand that fulfilling your commitments is an additional mark of success.

Your life is intense in the first couple of months of 2010, with a huge array of planets occupying your Sun sign. Pluto, Venus, the Sun, Mercury and the karmic north node combine to make this an extremely busy year. 'The more, the merrier', I say! You wouldn't have it any other way.

Jupiter passing through your zone of communication is also a lucky omen for you. Between the 8th of March and the 15th of April when the Sun, Venus,

Jupiter, Uranus and Mercury come into play, your words will have great power and you will be capable of achieving many things you thought were impossible. Do you call this luck? It's more a matter of timing just now, when many factors come together to provide you with one of the luckiest periods of your life in every respect.

Cupid smiles upon you in June when Venus joins company with a past karma point. Whatever good deeds you performed in your previous incarnations and earlier in this life, will now come back to you in the form of great company, opportunities for love, and possibly even marriage.

Venus blesses you with excellent opportunities and new friends around September, October and November. You'll feel at peace and increasingly confident in your ability to draw wonderful people into your life.

This must surely be one of the best years on record for you, Capricorn. Enjoy it to the fullest!

2010:
Month by Month
Predictions

JANUARY

*The most important single ingredient in the formula of
success is knowing how to get along with people.*

—Theodore Roosevelt

Highlights of the month

You are extremely motivated between the 1st and
the 3rd. The Sun activates your self-esteem as well
as your physical drive to achieve a whole lot during
the first month of the year. Your sense of integrity
will increase, along with the desire to obtain more
information about many different topics after the
5th. Seek out information on educational opportunities.

In your relationships, try not to be too obses-
sive about gaining your objective, particularly after
the 8th. You may be ruthless in your approach and
so confident that others could misinterpret this as
cockiness and arrogance. You can achieve what you
desire through the art of gentle persuasion, rather
than sheer brute force.

Career objectives are highlighted around the 9th, at which time you may become overly serious about a certain aspect of your work or an employer's interactions with you. Remember, being serious about your work and enjoying yourself are not mutually exclusive. Others may see you as being a little callous or not open to enjoying a bit of light-hearted fun. Relax a little more at this time.

Between the 10th and the 14th of January, you have a chance to unwind and enjoy the quiet and comfort of your own company and solitude. You may have had other ideas socially but on the spur of the moment you may choose to opt out of a few of the invitations that come your way during this time of the month.

Your reclusive manner may only be short-lived and, after the 15th, when a solar eclipse in your Sun sign of Capricorn takes place, you'll feel much of your subconscious energies being released. This is both a time of self-reflection and action based upon the new insights you gained into yourself and others.

Around the 18th, Jupiter, the benefactor of the zodiac, enters your zone of siblings, short travels, communications and contracts. Although not your friendliest planet, this still causes you to expand your vision, improve your skills and reconnect with all of these aspects and people within your life. Contractual arrangements should go well and this is a time to push for what you believe you're worth.

Excellent financial opportunities seem to be in order due to the presence of Venus in your zone of income between the 19th and the 23rd. If it's a pay rise you're after, this could be the best possible time to approach your employer to make it happen.

The 27th up till the 31st is one of the better times to pursue your romantic dreams. You'll be hyped up and ready to take advantage of any and every social engagement that is presented. You will also make quite an impression wherever you go. Don't be afraid to go out on a limb and try something different with a fashion item or two.

Romance and friendship

On the 1st and 2nd of January, you'll have to step out of your old patterns of communicating if you want to capitalise on this powerful phase of emotional and sexual attractiveness. You can develop friendships and take them to a new level, and this sets the trend for a powerful new phase in your love life.

The period between the 3rd and the 5th could be rather combative and, if someone in your life is taking it a little easier and expecting things to happen without any effort on their part, this could cause you to retaliate and demand much more from them. Overall, however, you'll be feeling confident about your friendships and love life generally.

From the 6th until the 11th you'll be feeling very wary of people and, even if they offer you compliments, you might feel as if they have some hidden agenda or ulterior motive. Your attitudes are certainly changing, but you mustn't 'throw the baby out with the bath water' and disregard everything, because some of the statements being made may actually be true and come from an honest space. Take each person on their own merits.

You are feeling intense, attractive and want to be taken seriously by your friends between the 12th and the 15th. You need to make a few modifications to your personal appearance and grooming if you're going to have the impact you'd like to have. There may be some shock value in this but you'll have to stick by your guns if one or two of your friends feel that the new look isn't quite to their liking.

After the eclipse of the 16th, you'll be probing into your own and others' personalities to get rid of those aspects of your relationships that have been weighing heavily upon your mind. Communications are good around the 18th and give you the chance to air your grievances to get to the bottom of any problems that have been lingering for sometime.

An exciting period is marked between the 20th and the 23rd. You may need some fun and romance in your life and you're likely to get it, due to the influence of the Moon and Uranus. This is also a very creative period and will provide you with ample entertainment and satisfaction, up to and including the 29th.

A short journey is necessary on the 31st.

Work and money

Between the 2nd and the 4th you can see the bigger picture and are likely to take a greater interest in researching the possibilities for your working life. This is an excellent time to do so and will set the trend for the rest of the year, both in your work and your finances.

Writing letters and communicating issues of business and finance on the 5th, 6th and 7th are important. Don't postpone these matters.

A 'new you' emerges in your business dealings around the 15th. You can see where you need to become a little harder in your attitude, even at the risk of alienating others. Professional change is also likely to be in the air, but you'll want to keep your plans under wraps.

Around the 18th, you may realise that what you have to offer is true, solid in its basis and able to change things for the better, but others may not agree. This is a case of silence being golden.

Health matters are tied in with work around the 25th. Don't overdo things, and if your body tells you to rest, do so.

Disputes with co-workers around the 30th can be avoided as long as you are open-minded in your responses.

Destiny dates

Positive: 1, 2, 19, 20, 21, 22, 23, 27, 28, 29, 31

Negative: 25

Mixed: 3, 4, 5, 6, 7, 8, 9, 10, 11, 12, 13, 14, 15, 16, 18, 30

FEBRUARY

Highlights of the month

Formulating new ideas to improve your personal relationships and your financial ambitions is strongly marked throughout February.

Although you are quietly confident about achieving some new milestones in your workplace career, you're also slightly nervous about the prospect of changes this month. Patience may be in short supply when you try to demand your ideas and schedules are implemented.

Between the 1st and the 4th, you'll be moving quickly, probably at a breakneck speed, and others might be unable to keep up with this hectic pace you've set as the benchmark. Remain sensitive to the capacity of others to keep up with you.

On the 6th your bills will be irritating; but remember they represent the many benefits you enjoy in contemporary life such as electricity, computing, the Internet, water, cars and other lifestyle perks. Change your thinking and see what a charmed life you really have.

You are forward thinking, visionary and also somewhat selfless during the period of the 7th to the 12th. You could be putting in long hours and this may impact upon your personal relationships. From the 15th to the 17th, you could expect some disputes over your inability to make sufficient time for the ones you love. If you're a family person, this may get rather uncomfortable, especially with the Sun being in close proximity to Neptune between the 15th and the 20th.

Your role in life—both as a family person, a friend or just as a human being—may start to become fuzzy and you'll need to think more carefully about the bigger picture. Openly communicate your feelings and don't bottle up your grievances otherwise you're likely to explode, bringing about some messy repercussions in your personal relationships.

Venus coming into contact with Jupiter on the 17th, and then the Sun also making a wonderful connection with jovial Jupiter as well on the 28th, are excellent omens for success, generosity and happiness all around. I can safely predict some wonderful new opportunities for you at this time, which may even include travel, new business contacts and/or employment interviews for a much-coveted position with better pay prospects. This is certainly a lucky time for you in 2010.

Maintain an optimistic attitude, especially after the 25th, when you might start to feel a little bored with your work or with circumstances generally, irrespective of how lucky the celestial patterns seem to be. Get that health check you've intended to have after this period so you can enjoy the remainder of the month.

Romance and friendship

You may want to escape the hustle and bustle of work and daily routine around the 2nd but may have family or possibly even work issues demanding too much of you. If your energy is low, you do need to at least make some effort to get to bed earlier and to also take a few additional vitamins to lift your energy levels again.

From the 3rd till the 8th you will be noticed by others, which pleases you immensely. Your social and personal agenda could be quite busy, and this is an excellent time to seek out new friends and people of like interests. Your social life will dominate your agenda for the time being and this will be exactly as you want it.

Around the 10th, you will be obsessed by some issue surrounding a friend or family member and must learn when to let go. In fact, you could be so emotionally charged that it will affect your health. What's this drama telling you? Learning the art of acceptance will be one of the major life lessons that could arise around this time.

If your family life seems a little bit heavy between the 11th and the 14th, whatever confusion is at the heart of this oppressiveness can be lifted by kindness, compassion and selflessness on your part. You could also try entertaining your relatives rather than being too heavy handed. You'd be surprised at how easily you can defuse the situation and also have a few laughs at the same time.

You're unexpectedly lucky between the 15th and the 17th. A gift or some special gesture by a friend will instil confidence in you.

A hot and steamy love affair could arise between the 19th and the 24th. Maintain contact with your normal peer group, otherwise they could think you're using them for your own gains. Don't let relationships become a matter of convenience.

Your mind is on faraway things on the 28th and an opportunity for travel and also communication with people of a foreign disposition is indicated.

Work and money

Between the 2nd and the 5th, there's an increased mode of agreement between you and your work colleagues. A team effort is needed, which will help all of you achieve your desired end. However, a rest on the 7th may be necessary to recharge your batteries.

Some confusion surrounding money between the 8th and the 10th is spotlighted but the difficulty is more or less in your own mind rather than the reality. Stop projecting your fears and you'll realise that the situation is not as bad as you think.

Contracts or verbal agreements are high on your list on the 14th. Don't be afraid to ask for what you feel is a fair deal, particularly if a heavier workload has been a feature of your working life. You can achieve a better position in your negotiations by speaking openly and honestly.

Between the 17th and the 20th, you needn't let a disagreement with a friend turn into a confrontation over money. In fact, it's better to be light-hearted about the topic rather than shoving your opinion in their face. You must agree to disagree over issues of money and/or politics.

Joint finances are pretty much a key focus between the 26th and the 28th. Speak about who owns what and who owes what.

Destiny dates

Positive: 5, 7, 21, 22, 23, 24, 25, 27, 28

Negative: None

Mixed: 1, 2, 3, 4, 6, 8, 9, 10, 11, 12, 13, 14, 15, 16, 17, 18, 20

Highlights of the month

Throughout much of the first part of the year, Mars spends its time in one of your most intimate horoscope zones: the zone of sexuality and deep emotional connections. It has a very important part to play in your relationships and makes you particularly prone to being hot-headed, passionate, and even demanding in your personal relationships.

Between the 2nd and the 6th, your demands may not be completely fulfilled, which can give rise to frustration over the coming months. Finding an adequate outlet for these unfulfilled desires is critical to you being able to make 2010 a much more fulfilling period of your life.

There are perfect opportunities to open up the lines of discussion between the 8th and the 12th. If you're in a long-term committed relationship, or married, much of the problem seems to be associated with your partner's financial concerns. There could be professional difficulties and a great deal of stress surrounding the payment of bills, mortgages and credit card expenses.

Rather than demanding what you want, this is an excellent period to show your support and serve your friend or lover in a way that will make them feel more secure for the future. You, Capricorn, more than any other star sign, know how to do that, being born under the category of earth. Use your skills to show others how to do it.

Educational prospects are prominent throughout March, with several planets triggering your curiosity and desire to expand your mental horizons. This month commences with a full Moon, occurring in your ninth zone of higher learning with Mercury, Jupiter, the Sun, Venus and Uranus all occupying the third zone of education as well.

No doubt, you will be keen to explore whatever avenues are available to you to improve your skill sets, not just for work and professional opportunities, but simply for the sake of learning about yourself, others and the world as a whole. This could be an extremely mind-expansive cycle in which you enjoy the company of other like-minded individuals. You therefore find yourself surrounded by many new and interesting people who can, over time, become friends and perhaps even lovers.

Between the 17th and the 20th of March an unexpected twist in your affairs makes life exciting but also a little harrowing. You need to get clarity on others' agendas as well as your own so that you can slot into one another's expectations.

From the 22nd to the 31st your attention will be fairly and squarely on your home affairs and dealing with issues on the home front. Spending quality time with your family will seem rather appealing.

Romance and friendship

Your mind is fast and agile between the 1st and the 4th, but you may also overreact and be too quick off the mark in assuming things. This could punch a hole in your confidence around the 2nd, but it's all a matter of listening more carefully to what others are saying before 'shooting from the hip'.

Exciting romances or something off-beat or completely out of character marks your relationships between the 5th and the 8th. You're on the lookout for a new experience, and somehow you may bump into someone who's looking for exactly the same thing.

Family members are intense on the 9th and so this requires you to be a little less so in your responses. You may be quizzed, interrogated and possibly even judged harshly by someone you thought accepted your views. Don't be too hard on them and don't do the same by judging them as severely as they have been judging you.

Communications, romance and increased social activity are marked for the period of the 13th to the 16th. You may take on a little too much so be prepared for a dose of divided loyalties, especially if you haven't managed your social diary particularly well.

An incident at home between the 17th and the 19th may cause a change of plans. Deal with it quickly and don't dwell on it after the matter has been resolved. Someone may want to keep luring you back into going over old ground. That would be a mistake. Let bygones be bygones.

You're feeling warm and fuzzy between the 20th and the 25th. Fuzzy could turn into sexy around the 26th, when your partner is more romantic than usual. Are you ready, willing and able?

The month finishes on a thoroughly positive and fun note, with the Moon transiting through your eleventh house of personal friendships and fulfilment.

Work and money

You could find it hard balancing the views, opinions and demands of co-workers and bosses with what you feel you need to achieve between the 1st and the 4th. It's a case of not being able to please everyone all of the time. You'll find a way, even if it means leaving someone a little disgruntled about your decision.

Low-key work should be anticipated between the 5th and the 8th, but don't be distracted by telephone calls or e-mails offering you a quick fix if boredom is setting in. Stay with it, do the job, even if you have to be alone for a couple of days. This will clear the decks and make you feel much more relaxed.

You'll spend a lot of time letter writing and

e-mailing or looking through newspapers and marketing advertisements between the 9th and the 14th. If you're looking to enhance your viability as an asset to some company or project, you need to get your résumé in order.

From the 17th until the 25th you should work harder. This will entail discarding the old to allow for the new to take root. Investigating technology or anything that can help improve your workplace practices is not a bad idea.

Speak to your boss on the 29th if you've got a problem with the way things are running. If you have a better system, they will be 'all ears'.

Destiny dates

Positive: 8, 9, 10, 11, 12, 22, 23, 24, 25, 26, 27, 28, 29, 30, 31

Negative: 1

Mixed: 2, 3, 4, 5, 6, 17, 18, 19, 20

Highlights of the month

Friendship takes on a special significance throughout April and on the 1st and the 2nd you could find yourself deepening your attachment to several people whom you've known for a while. Isn't it funny how you can know someone for so long but not really quite know them until one day comes along when—snap—something gives and you are able to appreciate their personalities, their gestures and other aspects of their lives just so much more? Well, this is what's likely to happen during April because friendships and love affairs are in the spotlight.

Between the 6th and the 12th, romantic energy is oozing from every pore of your skin. Singles born under the sign of Capricorn have excellent opportunities to meet and keep those they discover in a variety of social scenarios. With Venus transiting your fifth zone of love affairs, creativity and youngsters, expect this month to be full of fun, laughter, and creative as well as sexual impulses.

And let's not forget Mars, who is still transiting your zone of sexuality. If anything, you'll need to carefully plan your activities from the 14th till the 17th because you will find yourself overloaded with just a little too much to handle. Your passions will also need to be brought under some measure of control, due to the hard aspect between Mars, Venus and Mercury. Impulse is rife and you're likely to say or do something you'll later regret.

Lost love or an unresolved friendship from the past may resurface between the 18th and 20th. You'll either get pleasure from it or detest what transpires. You can't do anything about it, though, only learn from it. If you meet them head on, remain non-judgemental in your outlook. You will begin to see things differently in time.

You are able to reflect on your past, your actions and attitudes in the latter part of the month, especially after the 21st. Things may have moved way too quickly over the first two weeks of April, but now you have a chance to reflect and consider the ramifications of your actions.

Remember the saying 'It's far better to be safe than sorry'? Take precautions, will be your key words, especially between the 22nd and the 25th. Make every effort to understand strangers or people who come into your orb who may be demanding far too much and way too quickly. Get to know them before making any sort of commitment.

This advice I'm giving you should also be thoroughly extended to your business and financial affairs. Don't sign on the dotted line until you get clarification on the repercussions of any commitment that entails handing over money or other assets.

Romance and friendship

At some point you have to take a gamble on whether or not happiness is determined by your past conditioning or by choices that you make. You don't have to stay in a situation that is untenable and between the 1st and the 3rd you'll realise this and try to make some changes.

If you're accused of something on the 5th, trying to defend yourself may only make you look guiltier. Try to attack this from a different angle. Sometimes no amount of justification is going to convince the other person of your innocence.

You're looking at changing things in your life and, most importantly, yourself. From the 7th until the 12th you'll be interested in communicating with others who have some sort of insight into how you can spiritually, psychologically and possibly even physically change yourself. Educational pursuits, lectures and an attempt to connect with a life coach is an excellent use of your time in this period.

You're feeling young, funny and zestful between the 16th and the 18th. Seeking out younger people or at least those with younger attitudes will be important. A minor health issue on the 17th passes quickly, so don't make too much of it.

On the 19th and 20th, dealing with someone who is hypersensitive could be an issue. If you have something of value to say to them, even if in your view it's a constructive criticism, think twice before offering your opinion.

You can give good advice to a friend between the 22nd and the 25th, but don't expect them to take it. If you get angry at their lack of initiative, you've failed to understand how human beings work. Offer your advice and leave it at that. It's not your responsibility to make them implement it.

A friend could be secretive on the 28th and this will annoy you. Respect other peoples' privacy.

Work and money

You might not feel so lucky between the 6th and the 8th, but if you change your attitude you'll realise that luck is simply a matter of application and timing coinciding. Learn to trust the process and keep working with an attitude of love and gratitude.

There could be some confusion over your pay and finances between the 10th and the 12th. Try to be clear in the way you negotiate or hand over money. You could be short-changed.

A temptation to speculate is strong between the 15th and the 20th. However, take care around the 17th that you don't actually act on an impulse and spend money without adequate research, especially if this relates to the stock market or other get-rich-quick schemes.

Your working environment could be in a state of flux between the 22nd and the 29th. You have to stick to your game plan rather than being swayed by the opinions of others. On the 30th, someone may leave your place of work and you could feel as though a valuable asset and ally has disappeared. Take heart because the universe will quickly replace that loss.

Destiny dates

Positive: 1, 2, 9, 21

Negative: 5, 26, 27, 28, 29, 30

Mixed: 6, 7, 8, 10, 11, 14, 15, 16, 17, 18, 19, 20, 22, 23, 24, 25

Highlights of the month

You can't please everyone all of the time, Capricorn, but you may be trying to do just that throughout the month of May, especially in the first three or four days. Between the 1st and the 3rd you'll realise that bending over backwards is no assurance you're going to be appreciated for what you do. Perhaps doing a little less and directing those efforts to people who are more grateful would be in order, don't you think?

This month sees a cloud hanging over your head financially. Mars moving forward and at a quicker pace in your zone of shared resources will make a strong contact in the coming few weeks with Neptune, the planet of idealism and sometimes confusion. I'd recommend that during the period of the 5th to the 10th, you take time to study your finances more carefully rather than sweeping any problems under the rug. Playing ostrich, burying your head in the sand, when you know that things have to be rectified, is not the way to go. But why is this happening, anyway? You are a Capricorn and that sort of behaviour is certainly out of character for you, wouldn't you say?

No, the best approach is to seek the appropriate advice to clarify any confusion you have financially. This may be a month where you discover, much to your satisfaction, that some of these problems are going to work in your favour. As an example, you may have been paying more on your bills than you should have been charged. Taking a little bit of time to sift through your bills, do the arithmetic and calculate whether or not you've been short-changed will, I feel, work in your favour in the long run.

You'll experience a little relief from the 16th till the 20th. Saturn will have made its way out of your professional sector, giving you a break for a time. This means the pressure of responsibility is off you and, although you may have to serve a few masters in your workplace, you'll be able to do it at a more leisurely pace without the pressure of deadlines that you know you can't possibly meet.

This month gives you the opportunity to clean up your office space, have a spring-clean at home and create a nicer sort of ambience in those areas of your life where you probably spend more hours than anywhere else. Feng shui, the dynamics of living and personal space, impacts upon your mental, emotional and spiritual health. You'll be doing yourself a favour to look into this.

From the 27th till the 30th you'll be keenly

interested in cooking, diet and other methods by which you could improve your health but also enjoy yourself at the same time. Sign up to the gym and/ or that cooking course to start feeding yourself healthier foods from now on.

Romance and friendship

Opposition and blockages are usually nature's way of making you stronger and more resilient. But you have to be flexible between the 2nd and the 7th. You may be feeling as if digging in your heels is the way to get your own way. But be pliable and listen with your heart rather than your ears. This is the secret of improving your relationships rather than making them worse.

If you've been feeling as if a decision has been delayed, you'll get good news after the 12th when Mercury moves forward. With the Moon also moving through your zone of love affairs on the same day, some positive information will come your way. Don't be too proud to pick up the phone and be the first one to make the call.

Between the 14th and the 20th, if you try to make too much of an impression, you could come across appearing fake and insincere. The top secret for popularity and success in life and love is to be transparent, sincere and in tune with your true values.

It's likely that a new fitness program will be inviting, not just for your health but to boost your social networking skills. This is a way you can kill two birds with one stone and it would be ideal to investigate the idea between the 21st and the 25th, during which time you have an opportunity to expand your circle of influence socially.

You have spiritual inclinations between the 26th and the 30th. You should follow your heart and trust your intuition. Some of the inner promptings you perceive will be spot on, especially in your appraisal of other people. If you don't feel comfortable about being in the company of someone, walk away.

Work and money

You don't like the idea of relying on other people for your financial security but sometimes it is better to gamble with other people's money than your own. Look into the principle of OPM; that is, Other People's Money.

During the period of the 2nd up until the 7th, you may not have the stability to use your own money for some business concept or project. Look into this more carefully to understand what resources and possibilities are available to you.

After the 12th, you have the green light to sign on the dotted line and this could be for a work-related contract, a purchase of some sort or simply an agreement that relates to the exchange of money for services. Don't nitpick and trust that Mercury will now give you the go ahead.

Creating new partnerships between the 17th and the 20th mustn't be done on a handshake. You need to ask the right questions, and even if you get a rather blunt response to enquiries, don't budge. Business should always be done formally and with proper advice.

Avoid unexpected surprises, especially with respect to your banking and mortgage issues; try to take a more hands-on approach. Schedule a meeting with your bank manager between the 30th and the 31st to iron out any misconceptions or doubts you have about your existing payment plan or contractual status.

Destiny dates

Positive: 1, 12, 21, 22, 23, 24, 25, 26, 27, 28, 29

Negative: 4

Mixed: 2, 3, 5, 6, 7, 8, 9, 10, 14, 15, 16, 17, 18, 19, 20, 30, 31

Highlights of the month

The celestial vibrations for your home life, your inner peace of mind and your relationships with parents and other family members are wonderful due to the entry of Jupiter into your domestic zone.

Around the 4th you'll be feeling comfortable about staying in and may not want to socialise as much as usual. Feeling safe in your haven, your castle, will give you a sense of security and an opportunity to reconnect with your loved ones.

Between the 10th and the 12th there may be some changes in your home life, which may relate to someone coming or going. Some Capricorns may make a sudden decision to change residence, to travel or to perhaps look at the potential of investing money in real estate. In any case, your home life, where you live and spend much of your personal time, will be spotlighted throughout June.

If you happen to be of marriageable age and have been in an extended relationship, you may start to become impatient about tying the knot. You must curb these impulses because that's precisely the sort of behaviour that may scare off a potential soulmate. Take your time and rest assured that if you're right for each other, things will come together.

These energies are on the increase from the 21st to the 25th, again highlighting the possibility of travel, a change of residence or shifts and fluctuations in the nature of your most important personal relationships. Don't turn a blind eye to the needs of your loved ones and friends because this could have a crucial bearing on the outcome of your relationships.

You have the travel bug again and this is due to the fact that Mars is transiting through your ninth zone of long-distance travels. The lunar eclipse on the 26th in your Sun sign also has a huge emotional charge about it. You may opt to 'throw all cares to the wind' and impulsively travel to a destination, known or unknown, simply to get away from it all. However, don't be rash because the upcoming conjunctions of Mars and Saturn could make you regret some of this rather impulsive behaviour, which is again not at all in keeping with your true Capricornian nature.

It's always a good policy to say less than necessary. Between the 28th and the 30th, this maxim will hold you in good stead, particularly if you have some legal or bureaucratic issues bothering you. Try not to react verbally; listen to the other person's viewpoint and then, if you must, posture quietly and assertively to get your way.

Romance and friendship

You may have a desire to move ahead, go it alone and reinforce your independence, especially after the 4th. You have a great deal of optimism and that's evidenced by the Moon conjoining Jupiter around the 6th. Around this time and up to and including the 8th, this desire for independence could rub up people the wrong way. Your relatives and other usual friends might be accustomed to you reacting in a certain way and could feel rather put out at this new attitude of yours. Oh well, they'll just have to get used to it.

Your creative and romantic feelings peak around the 9th and, by the 13th, your spontaneity could be a valuable asset to any friendship or deeper, more intimate relationship.

Sexuality and playful interactions with someone you love on the 14th and 15th really bring the joy back into your life and instil yet further confidence in the potential of the relationship.

Differences in your philosophical or religious views may become a sticking point between the 17th and the 19th. Try not to look so much at the differences in your relationships but rather at the similarities.

You could be feeling a little flat on the 19th due to some inhibited desire. Perhaps you've become a little too accustomed to freewheeling independence and someone is clipping your wings.

If you've had a temporary separation from your spouse or partner, some good news or unexpected contact after the 25th will ensure that their love is still real. The lunar eclipse on the 26th is also a highlight that can bring up a few secrets or unexpected truths between you and your most significant other.

Work and money

Listening to too much advice from too many different directions can be confusing. Sooner or later, you need to rely on your own capacity to make financial and professional decisions. Trust your own thought processes between the 1st and the 6th. You'll start to rely more on yourself when you see just how accurate your own assessments are becoming.

You can gain leverage over others by using your power, but this is more a misguided use of energy than a deliberate direction of your forcefulness between the 7th and the 11th. You need to maintain the support of those who would normally assist you. Therefore, consider sharing power and responsibility and remember, of course, a team effort usually rewards everyone in the process for their long-term interests.

A 'wolf in sheep's clothing' may pass your way around the 24th or 25th. Be mindful of those who are out to use you for what you have to offer. A lunar eclipse around the 26th reveals much about others and could, in its own way, help you to sidestep around a rather unsavoury character.

Destiny dates

Positive: 1, 2, 3, 4, 5, 7, 8, 9, 10, 11, 12, 13, 14, 16, 21, 22, 23

Negative: 17, 18, 19

Mixed: 6, 24, 25, 26, 28, 29, 30

Highlights of the month

Things can never go back to the way they were, is a key piece of wisdom you need to accept and take on board during July. Mercury and the karma points in your horoscope indicate you're trying to turn back the hands of the clock, of time. The key attitude to help your relationships move forward, especially between the 5th and the 9th, is one of acceptance and adjustment to the changes that your partner and friends are experiencing.

Changes like this require flexibility in your personality. A breadth of vision will allow you a deep insight into the fact that everyone is evolving but sometimes not at the same rate of change. This simple process of acceptance will make such a difference to your relationships.

By the 10th you'll feel much more intimate with your loved ones and there is a strong sexual flavour to the energies of Venus. You'll want to express yourself through tangible, demonstrative gestures and physical touching, and this will further enhance your relationships. However, just be mindful of the fact that, if you're in the company of strangers, do not invade their personal space, no matter how innocent you believe your physical gestures are.

An important development may take place, either in a personal relationship or with a business association around the 12th. This will set the trend for the appearance of new pathways in your life and, depending on how you handle the circumstances, your success is pretty much assured.

This also indicates some very positive benefits through an association with those who have money, power and great connections for you. Now, when I say this, I don't necessarily mean you need to be mixing with high-level business executives, but connections are indeed everything. Some introductions may take place that can help shortcut your way to the specific goal you have in mind. Remember, it's who you know, not always what you know.

You need to backtrack over old ground with a parent this month. After the 17th, you may realise you've inadvertently ignored or overlooked important components of a discussion with either your mother or father. You may have even wondered why you've been given the 'hairy eyeball treatment', if you know what I mean. Attention to detail is necessary, not just in the tactical affairs of finance, work and your daily routine, but also in the emotional affairs of the heart. Family comes first this month, don't forget that, Capricorn.

As Mars conjoins your ruling planet Saturn on the 31st in your zone of profession, you can expect the going to get a little tough for a while. Don't be deterred by the challenges that life throws you, but stand up, be counted, and accept your responsibility stoically, with a smile. This is the way to move forward and capitalise on the opportunities now presenting themselves to you.

Romance and friendship

Between the 1st and the 4th, you could suddenly be feeling infatuated, but this is only because you're wearing rose-coloured glasses when looking at others. You have some tempestuous mood swings at this time and the best course of action is to take off those glasses and see people as they are.

If you're able to look at things clearly, you can actually make a good decision about romance between the 6th and the 10th. Learning about another person's past and inner motivations would be a triumph in your love life.

A solar eclipse takes place in your marital zone on the 12th. This is an important development for your love life romantically. It will reveal what responsibilities and concessions are necessary to find happiness in your love life, whether or not you are attached or single. You may now find that someone around you is a perfect role model, who you can look up to and learn much from, if you are to improve this part of your life.

You're more synchronised with your peer group between the 14th and the 19th. There's a feeling that your interests are mutual and you are gaining much more from your friends at this time. Your heart and head could be working together, and this will also seem to open up more useful connections in your social network.

Jupiter moves into its retrograde phase from the 23rd. Making some important changes in your domestic life will be essential now but not necessarily easy. Going back through your past and re-appraising yours and others' actions are all key ingredients in making the right decision.

It will be wise not to let frustrations block your interactions on the 31st. Don't try to act as a mediator for a battle between others where no one will come out a winner.

Work and money

It's a good idea to clear the backlog of work early in the month, especially between the 3rd and the 8th. You'll need extra time to deal with some of the more pressing issues later in July.

Educational pursuits for the purpose of increasing your work's skill sets are evidenced by the movement of Venus through your zone of higher education after the 10th. Between the 12th and the 16th, seriously consider increasing and expanding your mental horizon and abilities. This will hold you in good stead if you're looking to earn a bigger salary or gain a better position.

Saturn's influence on your zone of professional activity, employers and self-esteem indicates a greater burden of responsibility and possibly even some frustration after the 22nd. This is a key period of your working life and indicates that your health, mental clarity and purposefulness will be essential in overcoming some frustrations that are building up to the 31st. Have a clear objective in mind. Plan your work and then work your plan.

Destiny dates

Positive: 10, 14, 15, 16, 18, 19
Negative: 22, 23, 31
Mixed: 1, 2, 3, 4, 5, 6, 7, 8, 12, 17

Highlights of the month

It's not necessary to push too hard to achieve what you have in mind, Capricorn. The conjunction of Mars and Saturn is never an easy one but you have the strength and integrity to make these energies work for you. Between the 4th and the 8th you'll be pushing your agenda way too hard and will meet with considerable resistance. When those who resist you push back even harder, you'll become brittle and may break.

There's an old proverb that says, 'In a powerful hurricane, the tall tree breaks but the blade of grass sways'. In other words, standing tall and firm and remaining inflexible is not always in your best interests. The blade of grass knows how to sway and adjust itself to the circumstances. In like manner, especially if you're a professional working with others (particularly hard-nosed business people), adjust yourself to their needs, bite your tongue and don't retaliate. This is the way forward.

If you haven't got the requisite skills to converse with people who seem to know much more than you do, you don't necessarily have to educate yourself formally. The combination of Mercury and Venus prove that you can extend your level of knowledge by reading more, watching the proper sorts of educational documentaries on television and mixing with people who are not your normal peer group. Don't be afraid to step outside your comfort zone in August, especially between the 11th and the 15th. You'll not only enjoy the company of many new and interesting people but land yourself an unexpected education of sorts.

Between the 16th and the 18th there are indications that your cultural horizons will also expand. Now, this doesn't necessarily mean you'll travel, but somehow I see a connection with foreigners, those who are not from your neck of the woods, so to speak, but who do have a wealth of experience, who themselves have travelled and are more than happy to share their experiences with you.

The full Moon in your finance zone on the 22nd is telling on your monetary status and your attitudes to the dollars and cents this month. You may have a stark realisation that money is simply a representation of your own time and the effort you exert to make it. You'll begin to realise that placing too much emphasis on these aspects of money is not exactly the correct way of dealing with it.

Get rid of your scarcity mentality and realise that money is a form of energy. In other words, more of it will flow your way if you don't focus too much on 'it' but rather on satisfying yourself through the actions you perform, through doing work you love, and through sharing your resources with the ones you love. These insights are very important as part of your growth process throughout 2010.

Romance and friendship

You can make a show of your feelings between the 2nd and the 5th and receive the perfect response from a potential lover or partner. You'll be received well and by the 7th will want to partner up with someone who's out and about, adventurous and ready to take a short journey with you.

Between the 8th and the 11th, don't be afraid to mix business with pleasure. Social activities could be strongly tied in with your professional life. Workplace seminars and social engagements relating to the products and services of your company might give you ample opportunity to meet someone who finds you very appealing. Between the 13th and the 15th, don't be too outgoing or honest about your feelings in public. People may misinterpret what you're saying and find you a little too forward.

Your passion is exceedingly strong between the 21st and the 27th. Venus and Mars bring you an extra dose of physical lust and excitement. You can either act upon this or bottle it up. Either way, you could feel as if you're 'between a rock and a hard place' during this time.

You could feel risky around the 28th. Believing

that the grass is greener on the other side may be based more on impulse than clear-headed thinking. Consider the repercussions.

You'll be feeling domesticated and homebound on the 29th and the 30th. Enjoy the time you have with family and make an extra effort to let them know you care. This is a time of bonding and an opportunity for you to reconnect with someone whom you feel doesn't quite understand you the way they used to.

Work and money

At work, procrastination between the 6th and the 9th of August could cripple you and even cause you to lose some important opportunities. You can't afford to lose momentum, which means you should call on others to give you some assistance if that can help your cause.

Take the initiative between the 11th and the 13th because this is a time when others will feel happy to follow your lead. There's a resurgence of vitality and initiative in you, which will inspire others to rally around to give you the much-needed support you are after.

Some advice you receive around the 14th may need to be re-evaluated if you're not going to take up the suggestion immediately. Consider the advice in the light of the circumstances at hand.

Between the 21st and the 30th you need to place important expenditures on hold because Mercury dictates that someone may 'throw a spanner in the works'. If you're not completely clear on the terms and conditions of a purchase, wait a little. It may be wise to have an exit strategy up your sleeve to feel confident when parting with money.

Destiny dates

Positive: 2, 3, 9, 10, 11, 12, 16, 17, 18, 29, 30

Negative: 6, 28

Mixed: 4, 5, 7, 8, 13, 14, 15, 21, 22, 23, 24, 25, 26, 27

Highlights of the month

You might feel washed out, out of shape and simply out of sync, not just with the people around you but even with yourself, around the 1st and the 2nd. The Moon is commencing its transit this month in your zone of health and vitality. Being in the sign of Gemini, it's important for you to keep warm, protect yourself against the elements and don't overwork under any circumstances, even if you do have deadlines to meet.

Your communication lines could be affected by interference this month and as a result the period of the 6th to the 11th, in particular, might not go as well as you planned. Knowing this, you are forearmed. Take extra precautions to explain your position, to gain clarification on the time, date and place of your meetings.

There's nothing more frustrating than misunderstanding one word or two in a direction. It can throw a whole appointment out of whack. A little more diligence is necessary to help you sidestep impending misunderstandings and possibly even arguments.

Your popularity will increase this month, so don't worry too much about the previous statements. Just keep them in the back of your mind. I'm always pleased to see Venus moving through the zone of friendships, and this occurs around the 9th when it makes itself felt in all aspects of your friendships, social alliances and even workplace arrangements. Now you can gain great benefits through using your charm and your persuasiveness in any type of social engagement.

Venus also has some very positive material ramifications for you because the eleventh zone of your horoscope, through which it is travelling, represents the profitability of any business or financial enterprise. You can fulfil your material dreams this month and, in particular, if you happen to be a person running an independent venture, things are likely to go well with a boost in profits of the business itself.

This is also an excellent time to venture forth and create new alliances for yourself. Once again, as mentioned earlier in the year, connecting with those who have the wherewithal to introduce you to the right players in the game will make a marked impact on your profitability and overall success in 2010.

Finally, the separation of Mars and Saturn brings with it a huge sense of relief, and the connection of Venus tells us you're likely to feel an increasing amount of passion—and I don't mean only in the sexual or physical sense—but a passion and zest for life, work and quality achievement. This is a wonderful conclusion to the month and indicates your mind is clear and once again focused on the 'job' of life itself.

Romance and friendship

You could be reaching for the stars in your romantic life, doing anything and everything to gain the respect and honour of someone whom you feel is worthy of your love, only to find you're not quite achieving the goals you had in mind. Between the 1st and the 7th, you could go through a whole series of feelings, including optimism, hope, despair, apprehension and sensuality. You need to synthesise all these feelings and direct such energies in the correct way to solve the riddle of love.

Between the 8th and the 10th, your excitement may calm down a little, giving you the chance to see and feel things more clearly. You may not feel quite as sexual or intimate with your partner but most certainly will have a clearer picture of what to do practically.

Between the 11th and the 14th, you are likely to be way too eager in your social or personal affairs and this will put you at a disadvantage. As a result, you could feel needy and therefore send out the wrong signals to others who feel as if you lack value. Your key phrase is 'grace and self-confidence' at this time.

You can get your message across on the 19th, which will help allay any doubts your friends have about where you stand. You're thinking outside the square now and this is a little unsettling to others, particularly family members. But they will certainly take notice of you, won't they?

You mustn't let people victimise you by calling the shots between the 23rd and the 30th. This is a week when you need to pull out the big guns and let everyone know you're in control. Sometimes, a little bit of posturing can save you an awful lot of time, Capricorn.

Work and money

There's an old saying that says, 'Clothes make the man'. That goes for women, too! Between the 3rd and the 9th, you may need to pay a little more attention to how your clothes, colours and other objects of fashion are impacting upon others' perceptions of you. By gaining more understanding of this side of non-verbal communication, you can greatly enhance your ability to do business, win the approval of others and thereby further your own interests professionally and financially.

You may appear more serious to others between the 8th and the 10th, but this is precisely what will win the approval of your employer at this time. There's every opportunity and likelihood of you gaining a better position, which will result in increased pay, especially when the Moon conjoins Venus around the 11th.

The 13th till the 16th is an important few days in which your decisions will be clear, concise and able to have impact on others. Moreover, your communication will be very persuasive, much to your advantage.

You have a desire to share some of your well-earned money and, between the 19th and the 23rd, you could even consider some humanitarian or charity organisation as a means of fulfilling your wish to share some of your wealth.

Destiny dates

Positive: 16, 19, 20, 21, 22

Negative: 24, 25, 26, 27, 28, 29, 30

Mixed: 1, 2, 3, 4, 5, 6, 7, 8, 9, 10, 11, 12, 13, 14, 15, 23

OCTOBER

Highlights of the month

The enthusiasm, vitality and passion from you that I discussed in September continues during October and the two planets, Venus and Mars, edge their way together through your zone of friendships and life fulfilment. If you've been sensing someone's attraction for you, you're probably correct.

Between the 1st and the 4th, Cupid's arrows may hit you directly in the heart—bullseye! But you mustn't be shy or doubtful about someone's intentions. If your intuition whispers in your ear that you have a good shot at love, at romance, then open your heart to the range of human possibilities and accept the invitation. This is no time to be playing mind games.

There could be some divided loyalties this month with an additional pair of planets, the Sun and Saturn, dominating the upper part of your horoscope that represents your career, employment and commitment. Around the 8th there may even be opportunities to 'ascend the throne'.

A promotion is likely but this could be received reluctantly because you realise an additional amount of time and effort will be required to fulfil the role. If you foresee yourself in a situation that won't make you feel happy, it's best to decline and not let your ego get the better of you.

Sudden flashes of luck and inspiration punctuate your affairs between the 10th and 17th, and you have Jupiter and Uranus to thank for that, being placed in your third zone of communication. But also, unknown to many, even to astrologers, this third house is lucky for lottery tickets, raffles and other games of chance.

With Venus and Mars also influencing the fifth zone of speculation, I daresay it would be worth taking a punt this month, especially between the 18th and the 24th. Who knows? You may just get lucky and find yourself the recipient of some additional cash or at least a hamper at the local club.

Your mental state has to be perfectly in tune with your bodily state from the 25th till the 27th. If you are hell-bent on doing something great in life, it will be wasted if your convictions aren't true. Why are you doing what you do? Is it to impress someone? Is it for glory and adulation? Or do you genuinely love what you are doing? If love is your motive, you're on the right path.

When Mars finally moves into your zone of secrets, hospitals and hidden activities on the 28th, you may need to extend yourself and show some compassion to someone who needs help. Make yourself available because the outcome of this is a wonderful sense of relief and spiritual upliftment for having participated. The key word in the last couple of days of the month is 'selflessness'.

Romance and friendship

You don't want to come across as too serious between the 1st and the 7th but, by the same token, you don't want others to take advantage of you. There could be a sense of growing responsibility and maturity about you during this first part of October and you could be giving off the wrong signals to others. Instead, you could use others as a form of marketing to spread the message out about how you feel and who you really are. Talk to a few close friends whom you know have big mouths and this will spread the word!

Venus and Mars again combine forces in your zone of friendships this month and things can hot up in this arena. Use their power to enjoy your life, make some new friends and even enjoy the spontaneous passion of the moment. By the time Mercury conjoins Saturn around the 8th, you could be feeling less communicative and may want others to do more of the talking.

Between the 10th and the 14th, a jam-packed social agenda is forecast. You could be rather anxious about how others will perceive you but your worst enemy is your own fear. Hold up your head and be yourself.

The new Moon around the 16th is an excellent omen for putting your best foot forward in relationships. You mustn't let the past encroach upon the way you deal with others. Someone you used to be involved with may come out of the woodwork and make you feel nervous. Use your unconventional wisdom to sidestep this encounter and continue to enjoy the situation.

Between the 28th and the 30th, you could find yourself in a compromising situation. If you've agreed to help someone to do something or be somewhere that eventually turns out to embarrassing, it will be hard to extricate yourself from it. A little bit of research and investigation beforehand might give you the 'heads up' before it's too late.

Work and money

You might be placing way too much emphasis on your earning capacity rather than your capacity to love what you do. Take some time to reconsider your direction between the 3rd and the 7th. You could well be making money but at the expense of your inner peace and creative satisfaction.

Venus, the planet ruling your career zone, moves into retrograde motion on the 8th and this indicates important changes could take place with respect to your career or workplace agreements. Being forewarned, you are forearmed, and need to take the necessary measures to avoid problems. Get proactive if you see something wrong, even if it involves your employer. Speak up but do it in a way that is not offensive.

The clever communications occurring between the 18th and the 25th open new doorways of opportunities for you. New contacts can help you achieve a coveted position by way of an introduction around the 26th. A quick change of plans after the 28th will be necessary to keep up with changing times.

Destiny dates

Positive: 15, 16, 17, 18, 19, 20, 21, 22, 23, 24, 25, 26, 27

Negative: 8, 29, 30

Mixed: 1, 2, 3, 4, 5, 6, 7, 8, 10, 11, 12, 13, 14, 28

Highlights of the month

Whatever confusion you've had regarding money will be cleared up, much to your satisfaction, between the 1st and the 4th. What's more, you'll find yourself the recipient of increased cash flow just when you need it, leading up to Christmas. Mercury, Venus and the Sun give you several opportunities or streams of income from which to draw upon, due to their presence in your zone of profitability.

The Moon also is not a bad omen, commencing its transit this month in your zone of fortune, luck and karma. This indicates that some of your good karma is ripening and likely to come back to you in the form of cold, hard cash, especially between the 5th and the 7th.

Venus on the 8th moves back into your professional zone, your area of self-esteem and your ego, indicating a boost to your public persona and the way others see you. You may choose to change your wardrobe, enhance your elegance and make others take note of you for who you are, not so much for what you do. You're still likely to do good work, and to bring to your activities a touch of style and creativity, for which Venus is well known.

Artistic pursuits seem to be high on your 'to do' list and you mustn't avoid going to that concert or art exhibition, or you yourself participating in some sort of creative or craft hobby. These things will help soothe your mind and give you a much-needed boost in energy, especially after the 16th.

Between the 19th and the 22nd it's 'all systems go' for a new relationship or friendship that previously you felt may have stalled. You might have given up on someone who took your phone number and didn't bother to call you in the first few days. But, much to your surprise, that long-awaited call may indeed come!

Hold onto your money and your personal belongings around the 23rd. Pay special attention to where you leave your valuables and, if possible, lock them away, especially if you have guests coming over whom you've not been familiar with before. Attention to detail is again an important aspect of short-circuiting losses and other financial problems.

The month ends with the return of Venus to your zone of friendship and fulfilment. Superb romantic opportunities take place on the 30th. You'll be feeling happy in your friendships and discussions you have with someone, which could make you feel very special.

Some of your personal goals may be high-lighted at this time. If you've had a hobby or a creative pastime that you haven't had much time for lately, this is an excellent period in which to recommit yourself to the path of beauty and artistic excellence.

Romance and friendship

A well-earned rest is quite likely to be the order of the day between the 1st and the 4th. You owe it to yourself to take some time out, especially if you've been bending over backwards to satisfy everyone else.

You feel sentimental between the 5th and the 7th but may not have that sentimentality reciprocated. As a result, you may need to put on a false face just to handle the situation. Don't let frustrations build up. You need to speak about how you feel.

You have a strong desire for travel, exploration and adventure between the 8th and the 11th. You could find yourself 'between a rock and a hard place' if your friend or partner is not in the same mood. Who said you can't travel alone? Are you adventurous enough to do it independently, is the question.

Many unresolved matters can come to a head around the 19th, with Jupiter and Venus giving you great energy to clear up confusions. On the same day, the Moon will make you emotional and able to take control of the situation without being too aggressive about it.

Don't be afraid to call for help between the 22nd and the 28th. Others are more than happy to help you understand your situation, especially if they have more experience in a certain area than you do. A wounded pride could be what's stopping you from reaching out to them. On the 30th, you'll be pleased to note someone extending their hand in friendship to reciprocate.

This is a month for resolving differences and for acting upon your own self-beliefs.

Work and money

You can manifest your visions at work after the 8th. This is an excellent time to use the powers of persuasion, your charm and other social skills to convince others of your suitability for a job or project. Behind-the-scenes activities, secret collaborations, rumour mongering and other subversive activities between the 9th and the 14th, strangely assist you in gaining a coveted position. This could involve a certain amount of undercover work to get the information you need.

If you are reckless with your wealth, you will quickly lose it, particularly between the 14th and the 21st. Make sure you've accounted for your money by keeping all your receipts, because it may be too late when you forget where and with whom you transacted.

Don't overlook an important principle in business—or friendships, for that matter—and that is to say thank you when someone does you a favour.

People could be forgiven for feeling as if you are using them as a means to an end if you don't show some appreciation for the contacts and business that they swing your way. This is likely to be an oversight on your part around the 26th or 27th.

Destiny dates

Positive: 1, 2, 3, 4, 5, 6, 7, 30
Negative: 9, 10, 11, 14, 15, 16, 17, 18
Mixed: 8, 19, 20, 21, 22, 23, 24, 25, 26, 27, 28

DECEMBER

Highlights of the month

On the 6th Uranus, the planet of innovation, foresight and abrupt but exciting events, moves forward and tells us that December is going to be anything but boring for you!

You are highly strung, edgy, but also able to contain your feelings and direct your energies into traditional and practical pathways to achieve a considerable amount leading up to Christmas. Mostly due to the positioning of the Sun and Mars in the quiet area of your horoscope, you should be able to do much of your work behind the scenes, especially in the first week of the month.

Between the 10th and the 14th, you can come out of your shell and blast apart any opposition to your plans, whether on the home front or in the workplace. Expect others to question your motivation but my suggestion for you is to stick to your guns. If you know you're right due to the huge amount of research that you've done on something, plough through it like a steamer through ice, and don't look back!

There may be some problems with people who want to undermine you throughout December and so you can expect the odd rumour or piece of gossip to head your way. Pay no attention to it and keep on working hard, up until the lunar eclipse on the 21st, which occurs in your zone of work and service. The truth will be revealed at this time, and you'll be vindicated. Silence is golden. You needn't retaliate or give weight to any of these rumour mongers.

Christmas on the 25th takes place with the Moon transiting out of your eighth zone of private and sexual matters into the ninth sector of philosophy, religion and higher ideals. What a perfect blend of the worldly with the spiritual. This should be a Christmas full of surprises, revelations and intensely good fortune.

As the year draws to a close, be aware of Mercury, the planet of quick-wittedness, humour and spritely, youthful vivaciousness. Humour will be your catchphrase as 2010 winds down. Use this to decompress any problems in your relationships and to usher in a thoroughly positive 2011.

With Venus continuing its transit through your zone of friendship, my clear forecast for you is that you'll be surrounded by many friends, relatives and genuine admirers. What a great end to an exciting year, Capricorn!

Romance and friendship

When passions are running high, it's easy to feel as if someone is absolutely perfect, which could be the case between the 1st and the 5th. Try to get a grip on yourself and look at things in a clear light. On the 6th, when a friend quietly pats you on the shoulder to point this out, you may not believe them. You should. They are probably seeing a person's character much more clearly than you.

You're not likely to drown in your emotions on the 7th and the 8th, but it's best to keep a lid on how you feel rather than sharing your thoughts too openly with others. This could be tantamount to social suicide! Keep your cards close to your chest.

You can settle old scores before Christmas and, in particular between the 14th and the 19th, speak to others about forgiveness and let go of old, hurtful resentments that are undermining your personal happiness. It's also not a bad idea to extend this openness to issues still hanging around with family members, maybe with your mother or older females in your family. On the 14th, 21st and 23rd, take the time to say sorry if you truly believe you've transgressed against someone in some way.

'Friendship' is the key word in the last few days of the month. Between the 28th and the 31st, you could find yourself in touch with friends whose positive sides of their characters you've previously overlooked. Forget the negativities of the past and try to foster the good in any of your relationships at the close of the year.

Work and money

Between the 1st and the 7th, you'll be disciplined about your work and want to clear the decks so you can thoroughly enjoy Christmas this year. Don't forget that you must balance your physical needs with getting your deadlines met.

You might not want to be with others, even if they're trying to be helpful, between the 6th and the 10th. You need to be diplomatic in hiding from them. It's in this period that some unique solutions are likely to be discovered by you and you'll want to take full credit for that as well.

You'll be relentless in your application of effort to get across the finishing line between the 14th and the 19th. Don't push too hard, however, because there is a tendency to injure or exhaust yourself through long hours and having a workaholic approach to your profession.

The lunar eclipse on the 21st is important in helping you understand your motivations for working and what truly matters in life. If you don't quite complete all your work, relax and enjoy Christmas and remember that you'll have plenty of time in 2011 to tidy up those loose odds and ends.

Destiny dates

Positive: 9, 10, 11, 12, 13, 20, 22, 24, 25, 28, 29, 30, 31

Negative: None

Mixed: 1, 2, 3, 4, 5, 6, 7, 8, 14, 15, 16, 17, 18, 19, 21, 23

2010:
Astronumerology

*The happiness and misery of men depend no less on
temper than fortune.*

—Francois de La Rochefoucauld

The power behind your name

By adding the numbers of your name you can see
which planet is ruling you. Each of the letters of
the alphabet is assigned a number, which is listed
below. These numbers are ruled by the planets.
This is according to the ancient Chaldean system of
numerology and is very different to the Pythagorean
system to which many refer.

Each number is assigned a planet:

AIQJY	=	1	Sun
BKR	=	2	Moon
CGLS	=	3	Jupiter
DMT	=	4	Uranus
EHNX	=	5	Mercury
UVW	=	6	Venus
OZ	=	7	Neptune
FP	=	8	Saturn
—	=	9	Mars

Notice that the number 9 is not aligned with a letter
because it is considered special. Once the numbers

have been added you will see that a single planet rules your name and personal affairs. Many famous actors, writers and musicians change their names to attract the energy of a luckier planet. You can experiment with the list and try new names or add the letters of your second name to see how that vibration suits you. It's a lot of fun!

Here is an example of how to find out the power of your name. If your name is John Smith, calculate the ruling planet by assigning each letter to a number in the table like this:

J O H N S M I T H
1 7 5 5 3 4 1 4 5

Now add the numbers like this:
$1 + 7 + 5 + 5 + 3 + 4 + 1 + 4 + 5 = 35$
Then add $3 + 5 = 8$

The ruling number of John Smith's name is 8, which is ruled by Saturn. Now study the name-number table to reveal the power of your name. The numbers 3 and 5 will also play a secondary role in John's character and destiny, so in this case you would also study the effects of Jupiter and Mercury.

Name-number table

Your name number	Ruling planet	Your name characteristics
1	Sun	Magnetic individual. Great energy and life force. Physically dynamic and sociable. Attracts good friends and individuals in powerful positions. Good government connections. Intelligent, impressive, flashy and victorious. A loyal number for relationships.
2	Moon	Soft, emotional nature. Changeable moods but psychic, intuitive senses. Imaginative nature and empathetic expression of feelings. Loves family, mother and home life. Night owl who probably needs more sleep. Success with the public and/or women.
3	Jupiter	Outgoing, optimistic number with lucky overtones. Attracts opportunities without trying. Good sense of timing. Religious or spiritual aspirations.

147

Your name number	Ruling planet	Your name characteristics
		Can investigate the meaning of life. Loves to travel and explore the world and people.
4	Uranus	Explosive character with many unusual aspects. Likes the untried and novel. Forward thinking, with many extraordinary friends. Gets fed up easily so needs plenty of invigorating experiences. Pioneering, technological and imaginative. Wilful and stubborn when wants to be. Unexpected events in life may be positive or negative.
5	Mercury	Quick-thinking mind with great powers of speech. Extremely vigorous life; always on the go and lives on nervous energy. Youthful attitude and never grows old. Looks younger than actual age. Young friends and humorous disposition. Loves reading and writing.
6	Venus	Delightful personality. Graceful and attractive character who cherishes friends

Your name number	Ruling planet	Your name characteristics
		and social life. Musical or artistic interests. Good for money making as well as abundant love affairs. Career in the public eye is possible. Loves family but is often overly concerned by friends.
7	Neptune	Intuitive, spiritual and self-sacrificing nature. Easily misled by those who need help. Loves to dream of life's possibilities. Has curative powers. Dreams are revealing and prophetic. Loves the water and will have many journeys in life. Spiritual aspirations dominate worldly desires.
8	Saturn	Hard-working, focused individual with slow but certain success. Incredible concentration and self-sacrifice for a goal.
		Money orientated but generous when trust is gained. Professional but may be a hard taskmaster. Demands highest standards and needs

to learn to enjoy life a little more.

9   **Mars**   Fantastic physical drive and ambition. Sports and outdoor activities are keys to wellbeing. Confrontational. Likes to work and play just as hard. Caring and protective of family, friends and territory. Individual tastes in life but is also self-absorbed. Needs to listen to others' advice to gain greater success.

Your 2010 planetary ruler

Astrology and numerology are very intimately connected. As already shown, each planet rules over a number between 1 and 9. Both your name *and* your birth date are ruled by planetary energies.

Add the numbers of your birth date and the year in question to find out which planet will control the coming year for you.

For example, if you were born on the 12th of November, add the numerals 1 and 2 (12, your day of birth) and 1 and 1 (11, your month of birth) to the year in question, in this case 2010 (the current year), like this:

$1 + 2 + 1 + 1 + 2 + 0 + 1 + 0 = 8$

The planet ruling your individual karma for 2010 will be Saturn because this planet rules the number 8.

You can even take your ruling name-number as shown earlier and add it to the year in question to throw more light on your coming personal affairs, like this:

John Smith = 8

Year coming = 2010

$8 + 2 + 0 + 1 + 0 = 11$

$1 + 1 = 2$

Therefore, 2 is the ruling number of the combined name and date vibrations. Study the Moon's number 2 influence for 2010.

Outlines of the year number ruled by each planet are given below. Enjoy!

1 is the year of the Sun

Overview

The Sun is the brightest object in the heavens and rules number 1 and the sign of Leo. Because of this the coming year will bring you great success and popularity.

You'll be full of life and radiant vibrations and are more than ready to tackle your new nine-year cycle, which begins now. Any new projects you commence are likely to be successful.

Your health and vitality will be very strong and your stamina at its peak. Even if you happen to have the odd problem with your health, your recuperative power will be strong.

You have tremendous magnetism this year so social popularity won't be a problem for you. I see many new friends and lovers coming into your life. Expect loads of invitations to parties and fun-filled outings. Just don't take your health for granted as you're likely to burn the candle at both ends.

With success coming your way, don't let it go to your head. You must maintain humility, which will make you even more popular in the coming year.

Love and pleasure

This is an important cycle for renewing your love and connections with your family, particularly if you have children. The Sun is connected with the sign of Leo and therefore brings an increase in musical and theatrical activities. Entertainment and other creative hobbies will be high on your agenda and bring you a great sense of satisfaction.

Work

You won't have to make too much of an effort to be successful this year because the brightness of the Sun will draw opportunities to you. Changes in work are likely and, if you have been concerned that opportunities are few and far between, 2010 will be different. You can expect some sort of promotion or an increase in income because your employers will take special note of your skills and service orientation.

Improving your luck

Leo is the ruler of number 1 and, therefore, if you're born under this star sign, 2010 will be particularly lucky. For others, July and August, the months of Leo, will bring good fortune. The 1st, 8th, 15th and 22nd hours of Sundays especially will give you a unique sort of luck in any sort of competition or activities generally. Keep your eye out for those born under Leo as they may be able to contribute something to your life and may even have a karmic connection to you. This is a particularly important year for your destiny.

Your lucky numbers in this coming cycle are 1, 10, 19 and 28.

2 is the year of the Moon
Overview

There's nothing more soothing than the cool light of the full Moon on a clear night. The Moon is emotional and receptive and controls your destiny in 2010. If you're able to use the positive energies of the Moon, it will be a great year in which you can realign and improve your relationships, particularly with family members.

Making a commitment to becoming a better person and bringing your emotions under control will also dominate your thinking. Try not to let your emotions get the better of you throughout the coming year because you may be drawn into the changeable nature of these lunar vibrations as well. If you fail to keep control of your emotional life you'll later regret some of your actions. You must blend careful thinking with feeling to arrive at the best results. Your luck throughout 2010 will certainly be determined by the state of your mind.

Because the Moon and the sign of Cancer rule the number 2 there is a certain amount of change to be expected this year. Keep your feelings steady and don't let your heart rule your head.

Love and pleasure

Your primary concern in 2010 will be your home and family life. You'll be finally keen to take on those renovations, or work on your garden. You may even think of buying a new home. You can at last carry out some of those plans and make your dreams come true. If you find yourself a little more temperamental than usual, do some extra meditation and spend time alone until you sort this out. You mustn't withhold your feelings from your partner as this will only create frustration.

Work

During 2010 your focus will be primarily on feelings and family; however, this doesn't mean you can't make great strides in your work as well. The Moon rules the general public and what you might find is that special opportunities and connections with the world at large present themselves to you. You could be working with large numbers of people.

If you're looking for a better work opportunity, try to focus your attention on women who can give you a hand. Use your intuition as it will be finely tuned this year. Work and career success depends upon your instincts.

Improving your luck

The sign of Cancer is your ruler this year and because the Moon rules Mondays, both this day of the week and the month of July are extremely lucky for you. The 1st, 8th, 15th and 22nd hours on Mondays will be very powerful. Pay special attention to the new and full Moon days throughout 2010.

The numbers 2, 11 and 29 are lucky for you.

3 is the year of Jupiter

Overview

The year 2010 will be a number 3 year for you and, because of this, Jupiter and Sagittarius will dominate your affairs. This is extremely lucky and shows you'll be motivated to broaden your horizons, gain more money and become extremely popular in your social circles. It looks like 2010 will be a fun-filled year with much excitement.

Jupiter and Sagittarius are generous to a fault and so, likewise, your open-handedness will mark the year. You'll be friendly and helpful to all of those around you.

Pisces is also under the rulership of the number 3 and this brings out your spiritual and compassion-ate nature. You'll become a much better person, reducing your negative karma by increasing your self-awareness and spiritual feelings. You will want to share your luck with those you love.

Love and pleasure

Travel and seeking new adventures will be part and parcel of your romantic life this year. Travelling to distant lands and meeting unusual people will open your heart to fresh possibilities of romance.

You'll try novel and audacious things and will find yourself in a different circle of friends. Compromise will be important in making your existing relationships work. Talk about your feelings. If you are currently in a relationship you'll feel an upswing in your affection for your partner. This is a perfect opportunity to deepen your love for each other and take your relationship to a new level.

If you're not yet attached to someone, there's good news for you. Great opportunities lie in store and a spiritual or karmic connection may be experienced in 2010.

Work

Great fortune can be expected through your working life in the next twelve months. Your friends and work colleagues will want to help you achieve your goals. Even your employers will be amenable to your requests for extra money or a better position within the organisation.

If you want to start a new job or possibly begin an independent line of business, this is a great year to do it. Jupiter looks set to give you plenty of opportunities, success and a superior reputation.

Improving your luck

As long as you can keep a balanced view of things and not overdo anything, your luck will increase dramatically throughout 2010. The important thing is to remain grounded and not be too airy-fairy about your objectives. Be realistic about your talents and capabilities and don't brag about your skills or achievements. This will only invite envy from others.

Moderate your social life as well and don't drink or eat too much as this will slow your reflexes and weaken your chances for success.

You have plenty of spiritual insights this year so you should use them to their maximum. In the 1st, 8th, 15th and 24th hours of Thursdays you should use your intuition to enhance your luck, and the numbers 3, 12, 21 and 30 are also lucky for you. March and December are your lucky months but generally the whole year should go pretty smoothly for you.

4 is the year of Uranus

Overview

The electric and exciting planet of the zodiac, Uranus, and its sign of Aquarius, rule your affairs throughout 2010. Dramatic events will surprise and at the same time unnerve you in your professional and personal life. So be prepared!

You'll be able to achieve many things this year and your dreams are likely to come true, but you mustn't be distracted or scattered with your energies. You'll be breaking through your own self-limitations and this will present challenges from your family and friends. You'll want to be independent and develop your spiritual powers and nothing will stop you.

Try to maintain discipline and an orderly lifestyle so you can make the most of these special energies this year. If unexpected things do happen, it's not a bad idea to have an alternative plan so you don't lose momentum.

Love and pleasure

You want something radical, something different in your relationships this year. It's quite likely that your love life will be feeling a little less than exciting so you'll take some important steps to change that. If your partner is as progressive as you'll be this year, then your relationship is likely to improve and fulfil both of you.

In your social life you will meet some very unusual people, whom you'll feel are especially connected to you spiritually. You may want to ditch everything for the excitement and passion of a completely new relationship, but tread carefully as this may not work out exactly as you expect it to.

Work

Technology, computing and the Internet will play a larger role in your professional life this coming year.

You'll have to move ahead with the times and learn new skills if you want to achieve success.

A hectic schedule is likely, so make sure your diary is with you at all times. Try to be more efficient and don't waste time.

New friends and alliances at work will help you achieve even greater success in the coming period. Becoming a team player will be even more important in gaining satisfaction from your professional endeavours.

Improving your luck

Moving too quickly and impulsively will cause you problems on all fronts, so be a little more patient and think your decisions through more carefully. Social, romantic and professional opportunities will come to you but take a little time to investigate the ramifications of your actions.

The 1st, 8th, 15th and 20th hours of any Saturday are lucky, but love and luck are likely to cross your path when you least expect it. The numbers 4, 13, 22 and 31 are also lucky for you this year.

5 is the year of Mercury

Overview

The supreme planet of communication, Mercury, is your ruling planet throughout 2010. The number 5, which is connected to Mercury, will confer upon you success through your intellectual abilities.

Any form of writing or speaking will be improved and this will be, to a large extent, underpinning your success. Your imagination will be stimulated by this planet, with many incredible new and exciting ideas coming to mind.

Mercury and the number 5 are considered somewhat indecisive. Be firm in your attitude and don't let too many ideas or opportunities distract and confuse you. By all means get as much information as you can to help you make the right decisions.

I see you involved with money proposals, job applications, even contracts that need to be signed, so remain as clear-headed as possible.

Your business skills and clear and concise communication will be at the heart of your life in 2010.

Love and pleasure

Mercury, which rules the signs of Gemini and Virgo, will make your love life a little difficult due to its changeable nature. On the one hand you'll feel passionate and loving to your partner, yet on the other you will feel like giving it all up for the excitement of a new affair. Maintain the middle ground.

Also, try not to be too critical with your friends and family members. The influence of Virgo makes you prone to expecting much more from others than they're capable of giving. Control your sharp tongue and don't hurt people's feelings. Encouraging others is the better path, leading to greater emotional satisfaction.

Work

Speed will dominate your professional life in 2010. You'll be flitting from one subject to another and taking on far more than you can handle. You'll need to make some serious changes in your routine to handle the avalanche of work that will come your way. You'll also be travelling with your work, but not necessarily overseas.

If you're in a job you enjoy then this year will give you additional successes. If not, it may be time to move on.

Improving your luck

Communication is the key to attaining your desires in the coming twelve months. Keep focused on one idea rather than scattering your energies in all directions and your success will be speedier.

By looking after your health, sleeping well and exercising regularly, you'll build up your resilience and mental strength.

The 1st, 8th, 15th and 20th hours of Wednesday are lucky so it's best to schedule your meetings and other important social engagements during these times. The lucky numbers for Mercury are 5, 14, 23 and 32.

6 is the year of Venus

Overview

Because you're ruled by 6 this year, love is in the air! Venus, Taurus and Libra are well known for their affinity with romance, love, and even marriage. If ever you were going to meet a soulmate and feel comfortable in love, 2010 must surely be your year.

Taurus has a strong connection to money and practical affairs as well, so finances will also improve if you are diligent about work and security issues.

The important thing to keep in mind this year is that sharing love and making that important soul connection should be kept high on your agenda. This will be an enjoyable period in your life.

Love and pleasure

Romance is the key thing for you this year and your current relationships will become more fulfilling if you happen to be attached. For singles, a 6 year heralds an important meeting that eventually leads to marriage.

You'll also be interested in fashion, gifts, jewellery and all sorts of socialising. It's at one of these social engagements that you could meet the love of your life. Remain available!

Venus is one of the planets that has a tendency to overdo things, so be moderate in your eating and drinking. Try generally to maintain a modest lifestyle.

Work

You'll have a clearer insight into finances and your future security during a number 6 year. Whereas previously you may have had additional expenses and extra distractions, your mind will now be more settled and capable of longer-term planning along these lines.

With the extra cash you might see this year, decorating your home or office will give you a special sort of satisfaction.

Social affairs and professional activities will be strongly linked. Any sort of work-related functions may offer you romantic opportunities as well. On the other hand, be careful not to mix up your work-place relationships with romantic ideals. This could complicate some of your professional activities.

Improving your luck

You'll want more money and a life of leisure and ease in 2010. Keep working on your strengths and eliminate your negative personality traits to create greater luck and harmony in your life.

Moderate all your actions and don't focus exclusively on money and material objects. Feed your spiritual needs as well. By balancing your inner and outer sides you'll see that your romantic and professional lives will be enhanced more easily.

The 1st, 8th, 15th and 20th hours on Fridays will be very lucky for you and new opportunities will arise for you at those times. You can use the numbers 6, 15, 24 and 33 to increase luck in your general affairs.

7 is the year of Neptune

Overview

The last and most evolved sign of the zodiac is

Pisces, which is ruled by Neptune. The number 7 is deeply connected with this zodiac sign and governs you in 2010. Your ideals seem to be clearer and more spiritually orientated than ever before. Your desire to evolve and understand your inner self will be a double-edged sword. It depends on how organised you are as to how well you can use these spiritual and abstract concepts in your practical life.

Your past hurts and deep emotional issues will be dealt with and removed for good, if you are serious about becoming a better human being.

Spend a little more time caring for yourself rather than others, as it's likely some of your friends will drain you of energy with their own personal problems. Of course, you mustn't turn a blind eye to the needs of others, but don't ignore your own personal requirements in the process.

Love and pleasure

Meeting people with similar life views and spiritual aspirations will rekindle your faith in relationships. If you do choose to develop a new romance, make sure there is a clear understanding of the responsibilities of one to the other. Don't get swept off your feet by people who have ulterior motives.

Keep your relationships realistic and see that the most idealistic partnerships must eventually come down to Earth. Deal with the practicalities of life.

Work

This is a year of hard work, but one in which you'll

come to understand the deeper significance of your professional ideals. You may discover a whole new aspect to your career, which involves a more compassionate and self-sacrificing side to your personality.

You'll also find that your way of working will change and you'll be more focused and able to get into the spirit of whatever you do. Finding meaningful work is very likely and therefore this could be a year when money, security, creativity and spirituality overlap to bring you a great sense of personal satisfaction.

Tapping into your greater self through meditation and self-study will bring you great benefits throughout 2010.

Improving your luck

Using self-sacrifice along with discrimination will be an unusual method of improving your luck. The laws of karma state that what you give, you receive in greater measure. This is one of the principal themes for you in 2010.

The 1st, 8th, 15th and 20th hours of Tuesdays are your lucky times. The numbers 7, 16, 25 and 34 should be used to increase your lucky energies.

8 is the year of Saturn

Overview

The earthy and practical sign of Capricorn and its ruler Saturn are intimately linked to the number

8, which rules you in 2010. Your discipline and far-sightedness will help you achieve great things in the coming year. With cautious discernment, slowly but surely you will reach your goals.

It may be that due to the influence of the solitary Saturn, your best work and achievement will be behind closed doors away from the limelight. You mustn't fear this as you'll discover many new things about yourself. You'll learn just how strong you really are.

Love and pleasure

Work will overshadow your personal affairs in 2010, but you mustn't let this erode the personal relationships you have. Becoming a workaholic brings great material successes but will also cause you to become too insular and aloof. Your family members won't take too kindly to you working 100-hour weeks.

Responsibility is one of the key words for this number and you will therefore find yourself in a position of authority that leaves very little time for fun. Try to make the time to enjoy the company of friends and family and by all means schedule time off on the weekends as it will give you the peace of mind you're looking for.

Because of your responsible attitude it will be very hard for you not to assume a greater role in your workplace and this indicates longer working hours with the likelihood of a promotion with equally good remuneration.

Work

Money is high on your agenda in 2010. Number 8 is a good money number according to the Chinese and this year is at last likely to bring you the fruits of your hard labour. You are cautious and resourceful in all your dealings and will not waste your hard-earned savings. You will also be very conscious of using your time wisely.

You will be given more responsibilities and you're likely to take them on, if only to prove to yourself that you can handle whatever life dishes up.

Expect a promotion in which you'll play a leading role in your work. Your diligence and hard work will pay off, literally, in a bigger salary and more respect from others.

Improving your luck

Caution is one of the key characteristics of the number 8 and is linked to Capricorn. But being overly cautious could cause you to miss valuable opportunities. If an offer is put to you, try to think outside the square and balance it with your naturally cautious nature.

Be gentle and kind to yourself. By loving yourself, others will naturally love you, too. The 1st, 8th, 15th and 20th hours of Saturdays are exceptionally lucky for you, as are the numbers 1, 8, 17, 26 and 35.

9 is the year of Mars

Overview

You are now entering the final year of a nine-year cycle dominated by the planet Mars and the sign of Aries. You'll be completing many things and are determined to be successful after several years of intense work.

Some of your relationships may now have reached their use-by date and even personal affairs may need to be released. Don't let arguments and disagreements get in the road of friendly resolution in these areas of your life.

Mars is a challenging planet, and this year, although you will be very active and productive, you may find others trying to obstruct the achievement of your goals. As a result you may react strongly to them, thereby creating disharmony in your workplace. Don't be so impulsive or reckless, and generally slow things down. The slower, steadier approach has greater merit this year.

Love and pleasure

If you become too bossy and pushy with friends this year you will just end up pushing them out of your life. It's a year to end certain friendships but by the same token it could be the perfect time to remove conflicts and thereby bolster your love affairs in 2010.

If you're feeling a little irritable and angry with those you love, try getting rid of these negative feelings through some intense, rigorous sports and physical activity. This will definitely relieve tension and improve your personal life.

Work

Because you're healthy and able to work at a more intense pace you'll achieve an incredible amount in the coming year. Overwork could become a problem if you're not careful.

Because the number 9 and Mars are infused with leadership energy, you'll be asked to take the reins of the job and steer your company or group in a certain direction. This will bring with it added responsibility but also a greater sense of purpose for you.

Improving your luck

Because of the hot and restless energy of the number 9, it is important to create more mental peace in your life this year. Lower the temperature, so to speak, and decompress your relationships rather than becoming aggravated. Try to talk with your work partners and loved ones rather than telling them what to do. This will generally pick up your health and your relationships.

The 1st, 8th, 15th and 20th hours of Tuesdays are the luckiest for you this year and, if you're involved in any disputes or need to attend to health issues, these times are also very good to get the best results. Your lucky numbers are 9, 18, 27 and 36.

CAPRICORN

2010:
Your Daily Planner

I'll go through life either first class or third, but never in second.

—Noel Coward

According to astrology, the success of any venture or activity is dependent upon the planetary positions at the time you commence that activity. Electional astrology helps you select the most appropriate times for many of your day-to-day endeavours. These dates are applicable to each and every zodiac sign and can be used freely by one and all, even if your star sign doesn't fall under the one mentioned in this book. Please note that the daily planner is a universal system applicable equally to all *twelve* star signs. Anyone and everyone can use this planner irrespective of their birth sign.

Ancient astrologers understood the planetary patterns and how they impacted on each of us. This allowed them to suggest the best possible times to start various important activities. For example, many farmers still use this approach today: they understand the phases of the Moon, and attest to the fact that planting seeds on certain lunar days produces a far better crop than does planting on other days.

In the following section, many facets of daily life are considered. Using the lunar cycle and the combined strength of other planets allows us to work out the best times to do them. This is your personal almanac, which can be used in conjunction with any star sign to help optimise the results.

First, select the activity you are interested in, and then quickly scan the year for the best months to start it. When you have selected the month, you can finetune your timing by finding the best specific dates. You can then be sure that the planetary energies will be in sync with you, offering you the best possible outcome.

Coupled with what you know about your monthly and weekly trends, the daily planner is an effective tool to help you capitalise on opportunities that come your way this year.

Good luck, and may the planets bless you with great success, fortune and happiness in 2010!

Getting started in 2010

How many times have you made a new year's resolution to begin a diet or be a better person in your relationships? And, how many times has it not worked out? Well, part of the reason may be that you started out at the wrong time, because how successful you are is strongly influenced by the position of the Moon and the planets when you begin a particular activity. You will be more successful with the following endeavours if you start them on the days indicated.

Relationships

We all feel more empowered on some days than on others. This is because the planets have some power over us—their movement and their relationships to each other determine the ebb and flow of our energies. And, our levels of self-confidence and sense of romantic magnetism play an important part in the way we behave in relationships.

Your daily planner tells you the ideal dates for meeting new friends, initiating a love affair, spending time with family and loved ones—it even tells you the most appropriate times for sexual encounters.

You'll be surprised at how much more impact you will make in your relationships when you tune yourself in to the planetary energies on these special dates.

Falling in love/restoring love

During these times you could expect favourable energies to meet your soulmate or, if you've had difficulty in a relationship, to approach the one you love to rekindle both your and their emotional responses:

January	18, 20, 23, 24
February	15, 16, 20, 24
March	29
April	16
May	14, 17, 18, 19, 20, 23
June	14, 15, 16, 20, 21
July	12
August	10, 13, 14
September	9, 21, 22
October	8, 18, 19, 20
November	14, 15, 16, 19, 20, 21
December	13, 17, 18

Special times with friends and family

Socialising, partying and having a good time with those whose company you enjoy is highly favourable under the following dates. They are excellent to spend time with family and loved ones in a domestic environment:

January	6, 26, 27
February	12, 13, 14, 15, 16, 20, 24
March	11, 21, 22, 29, 30, 31
April	8
May	15, 16, 17, 18, 19, 20, 23, 24
June	1, 2, 3, 11, 12, 14, 15, 16, 20, 21, 29, 30
July	8, 9, 12, 17, 18, 26, 27
August	5, 6, 9, 10, 13, 14, 22, 23, 24
September	1, 2, 5, 9, 10, 18, 19, 20, 30
October	3, 19, 20, 25, 26, 30, 31
November	3, 4, 14, 15, 16, 22, 26, 27
December	2, 9, 10, 11, 19, 20, 24, 25

Healing or resuming relationships

If you're trying to get back together with the one you love or need a heart-to-heart or deep-and-meaningful discussion with someone, you can try the following dates to do so:

January	12, 13, 14, 15, 21, 22, 23, 24, 25
February	6
March	6, 31
April	2, 7, 8, 12, 16, 19, 23, 24, 25, 26

May	10, 11, 12, 13, 14, 15, 16, 17, 18, 19, 20, 21, 22, 23, 24, 25, 26, 27, 28, 30
June	3, 8, 9, 10, 11, 12, 13, 14, 15, 16, 17, 21, 22, 23, 25, 26, 27, 28, 29, 30
July	1, 2, 3, 4, 5, 10, 11, 12, 13, 15, 16, 17, 18, 19, 20, 21, 22, 23, 28, 29, 30
August	1, 2, 3, 4, 5, 6, 9, 10, 13, 14, 15, 16, 20, 23, 25, 26, 27
September	2, 5, 9, 10, 13, 17, 18, 19, 20
October	1, 2, 3, 6, 12, 13, 14, 15, 20, 22, 23, 24, 25, 26, 27, 28, 29, 30, 31
November	3, 4, 5, 6, 7, 8, 9, 21, 27, 28, 29, 30
December	2, 3, 4, 6, 12, 13, 14, 17, 18, 19, 20, 21, 23, 24, 25

Sexual encounters

Physical and sexual energies are well favoured on the following dates. The energies of the planets enhance your moments of intimacy during these times:

January	1, 6, 7, 21, 22
February	6, 12, 13, 14, 20, 24
March	14, 15, 17, 18, 19, 30, 31
April	23, 24, 25, 26
May	9, 12, 14, 17, 18, 19, 20
June	3, 8, 9, 10, 11, 14, 15, 16, 20, 21, 29, 30
July	8, 9, 10, 11, 12
August	6, 10, 13, 14, 22, 23, 24

September	3, 4, 5, 6, 9, 10, 18, 19, 20, 21, 22, 30
October	1, 2, 3, 7, 8, 18, 19, 20, 23, 24, 28, 29, 30, 31
November	3, 4, 14, 15, 16, 19, 24, 25, 26, 27
December	2, 10, 11, 12, 13, 15, 16, 17, 19, 20, 22, 23, 24, 25

Health and wellbeing

Your aura and life force are susceptible to the movements of the planets—in particular, they respond to the phases of the Moon.

The following dates are the most appropriate times to begin a diet, have cosmetic surgery, or seek medical advice. They also indicate the best times to help others.

Feeling of wellbeing

Your physical as well as your mental alertness should be strong on these following dates. You can plan your activities and expect a good response from others:

January	2, 3, 4, 5, 6, 7, 11, 12, 13, 14, 16, 17, 18, 21, 22, 23, 24, 30, 31
February	1, 2, 7, 8, 15, 16, 17, 18, 19, 20, 21, 22, 23, 24, 25, 26, 27, 28
March	16, 17, 18, 19, 20, 22, 23, 24, 25, 26, 27, 28, 29
April	7, 13, 14, 16, 28
May	2, 11, 14, 25, 26
June	8, 22, 23, 26, 27, 28, 29, 30

July	4, 5, 8, 9, 12, 13, 14, 15, 16, 19, 20, 23, 24, 25
August	5, 6, 9, 10, 11, 12, 13, 15, 16, 20, 21
September	9, 10, 11, 12, 13, 16, 17, 21, 22, 24, 25, 28, 29, 30
October	3, 4, 5, 6, 7, 8, 9, 10, 13, 14, 15, 22
November	4, 5, 6, 10, 11, 19, 20, 21
December	7, 8, 17, 18, 28, 29

Healing and medicine

These times are good for approaching others who have expertise when you need some deeper understanding. They are also favourable for any sort of healing or medication and making appointments with doctors or psychologists. Planning surgery around these dates should bring good results.

Often giving up our time and energy to assist others doesn't necessarily result in the expected outcome. However, by lending a helping hand to a friend on the following dates, the results should be favourable:

January	1, 2, 3, 4, 6, 7, 8, 9, 11, 12, 13, 14, 15, 16, 17, 18, 19, 20, 21, 22, 23, 24, 26, 27, 28, 29, 30, 31
February	1, 5, 6, 9, 11, 12, 13, 14, 15, 16, 19
March	1, 2, 3, 4, 5, 8, 9, 10, 11, 12, 18, 19, 24, 25, 29
April	1, 3, 4, 5, 22, 26
May	4, 5

June	1, 2, 3, 9, 10, 17, 18, 22, 23, 24, 25, 29, 30
July	6, 7, 15, 16, 17, 18, 19, 21, 22, 23, 24, 25, 26
August	2, 3, 4, 11, 12, 17, 18, 19, 20, 21, 30, 31
September	6, 7, 8, 10, 11, 12, 13, 14, 15, 16, 17, 18, 26, 27, 28, 29
October	5, 7, 8, 9, 10, 11, 12, 13, 14, 15, 16, 17, 18, 19, 20, 21, 22, 23, 24, 25, 26, 28, 29, 30, 31
November	1, 2, 3, 5, 7, 8, 10, 11, 14, 15, 17, 18, 19, 22, 23
December	4, 5, 7, 8, 9, 10, 12, 13, 14, 16, 23, 24, 25, 26, 28, 29, 30, 31

Money

Money is an important part of life, and involves many decisions—decisions about borrowing, investing, spending. The ideal times for transactions are very much influenced by the planets, and whether your investment or nest egg grows or doesn't grow can often be linked to timing. Making your decisions on the following dates could give you a whole new perspective on your financial future.

Managing wealth and money

To build your nest egg it's a good time to open your bank account or invest money on the following dates:

January	1, 6, 7, 13, 14, 15, 18, 21, 22, 28, 29
February	3, 4, 9, 10, 11, 12, 13, 14, 15, 17, 18, 24, 25

March	2, 3, 9, 10, 16, 17, 18, 23, 24, 29, 30, 31
April	5, 6, 7, 13, 14, 19, 20, 21, 26, 27,
May	2, 3, 4, 10, 11, 17, 18, 23, 24, 30, 31
June	6, 7, 8, 13, 14, 19, 20, 21, 26, 27, 28
July	4, 5, 10, 11, 12, 17, 18, 23, 24, 25, 31
August	1, 7, 8, 13, 14, 20, 21, 27, 28, 29
September	3, 4, 9, 10, 16, 17, 23, 24, 25
October	1, 2, 7, 8, 13, 14, 15, 21, 22, 28, 29
November	3, 4, 10, 11, 17, 18, 24, 25
December	1, 2, 7, 8, 14, 15, 16, 21, 22, 23, 24, 29

Spending

It's always fun to spend but the following dates are more in tune with this activity and are likely to give you better results:

January	3, 4, 5, 6, 7, 8, 9, 10, 11, 12, 13, 14
February	3, 4, 5, 10, 19
March	8, 10, 11, 13, 14, 19
April	7, 8, 11, 12, 22
May	6, 7, 8, 9, 10, 11, 12, 13, 17, 18, 19, 20, 21, 22, 23, 24, 25, 26, 27, 28
June	1, 11, 12, 14, 16, 17, 19, 23, 25, 26, 27, 28, 29, 30
July	6, 7, 8, 23, 24, 25, 26, 27, 28, 29, 31
August	1, 2, 3, 4, 5, 15, 16, 17, 18, 19, 30, 31
September	1, 2, 3, 4, 17, 18, 19, 20, 21, 22, 23, 27, 28, 29, 30

October	4, 7, 12, 13, 14, 15, 16, 17, 18, 19, 27, 28
November	2, 3, 4, 25, 26, 27, 28
December	11, 22, 23

Selling

If you're thinking of selling something, whether it is small or large, consider the following dates as ideal times to do so:

January	18
February	12, 13, 14, 15
March	5, 6, 9, 14, 15, 16, 17, 18, 19, 21
April	1, 3, 4, 5, 22, 26
May	7, 12, 21, 29
June	3, 8, 9, 10, 11, 12, 13, 17, 24, 25, 26, 27, 28, 30
July	1, 2, 7, 9, 10, 11, 25, 27, 28, 29, 30, 31
August	1, 2, 3, 4, 5, 6, 7, 8, 9, 10, 13, 20, 23, 28
September	2, 9, 10, 11, 12, 13, 14, 15, 16, 17, 18, 19, 20, 21, 22, 23, 24, 26, 30
October	1, 2, 3, 4, 6, 7, 10, 11, 17, 18, 19, 20, 21, 22, 23, 24, 25, 27, 29
November	3, 4, 5, 6, 7, 11, 14, 15, 16, 17, 18, 19, 21, 23, 24, 25, 26, 27, 28, 29, 30
December	1, 2, 3, 4, 5, 6, 7, 8, 9, 10, 11, 12, 13, 14, 15, 16, 17, 18, 19, 20, 21, 22

Borrowing

Few of us like to borrow money, but if you must, taking out a loan on the following dates will be positive:

January	12, 30
February	7, 12, 13
March	6, 7, 8, 11
April	3, 4, 8
May	9, 28, 29
June	1, 2, 3, 4, 5, 29, 30
July	1, 2, 3, 26, 27, 28, 29, 30
August	9, 25, 26
September	5, 6
October	3, 30
November	26, 27
December	3, 4, 21, 22, 23, 30, 31

Work and education

Your career is important, and continual improvement of your skills is therefore also crucial professionally, mentally and socially. The dates below will help you find out the most appropriate times to improve your professional talents and commence new work or education associated with your work.

You may need to decide when to start learning a new skill, when to ask for a promotion, and even when to make an important career change. Here are the days when your mental and educational power is strong.

Learning new skills

Educational pursuits are lucky and bring good results on the following dates:

January	15, 16, 17, 18, 19, 20, 21, 22, 25, 26, 27
February	14, 15, 16, 17, 18, 19, 22, 23, 28
March	16, 17, 18, 21, 22, 27, 28
April	17, 18, 24, 25
May	15, 16, 21, 22
June	12, 17, 18, 24, 25
July	15, 16, 21, 22, 23, 24, 25
August	11, 12, 17, 18, 19
September	8, 13, 15, 20, 21, 22
October	11, 12
November	7, 8, 9
December	6, 19, 20

Changing career path or profession

If you're feeling stuck and need to move into a new professional activity, changing jobs could be done at these times:

January	6, 7, 15, 16, 17, 23, 24
February	12, 13, 14, 19, 20, 21
March	19, 20, 27, 28
April	15, 16, 24, 25
May	14, 21, 22
June	17, 18, 19, 20, 21
July	8, 9, 15, 16, 23, 24, 25

August	5, 6, 11, 12, 20, 21, 22, 23
September	1, 2, 8, 13, 14, 15, 17
October	8, 13, 14, 15, 16, 17
November	3, 4, 10, 11, 19, 20, 21
December	1, 2, 3, 7, 8, 17, 18, 28, 29

Promotion, professional focus and hard work

To increase your mental focus and achieve good results from the work you do; promotions are also likely on these dates:

January	4, 5, 6, 11, 12, 13, 14, 15, 16, 17, 18, 19, 21
February	6
March	16, 17, 18, 19, 20, 21, 23, 24, 25, 26, 27, 28, 29
April	8, 28, 29
May	12, 21
June	25, 26, 27, 28
July	4, 5, 8, 9, 12, 13, 14, 15, 16, 17, 18, 19, 20, 21, 22, 23, 24, 25, 26, 27
August	5, 6, 10, 11, 12, 13, 14, 15, 16, 17, 18, 19, 20, 21, 22, 23, 24
September	13, 14, 15
October	10, 11, 12, 13, 14, 15, 17, 18, 19, 20, 22, 23, 24, 30, 31
November	2, 4, 5, 6, 7, 8, 9, 23, 24, 25, 26, 27, 28, 29, 30
December	2, 3, 4, 11, 12, 13, 14, 15, 16, 18, 19, 20, 21, 23, 24, 25

Travel

Setting out on a holiday or adventurous journey is exciting. Here are the most favourable times for doing this. Travel on the following dates is likely to give you a sense of fulfilment:

January	15
February	15, 16, 18, 19, 20, 21
March	16, 17, 18, 21, 22, 23
April	19, 24, 25, 26, 27
May	16, 17, 18, 21, 22
June	17, 18, 19, 20, 21, 24, 25
July	21, 22, 23, 24, 25
August	19
September	9, 21, 22
October	18, 19, 20, 21, 22
November	7, 16, 17, 18
December	6, 14, 16, 19, 20

Beauty and grooming

Believe it or not, cutting your hair or nails has a powerful effect on your body's electromagnetic energy. If you cut your hair or nails at the wrong time of the month, you can reduce your level of vitality significantly. Use these dates to ensure you optimise your energy levels by staying in tune with the stars.

Hair and nails

January	1, 2, 3, 4, 5, 6, 7, 8, 11, 12, 13, 14, 15, 18, 19, 20, 21, 22, 25, 26, 27
February	3, 4, 5, 7, 8, 15, 16, 17, 18, 19, 22, 23, 24, 25
March	2, 3, 4, 6, 7, 8, 14, 15, 21, 22
April	1, 2, 3, 4, 5, 10, 11, 12, 17, 18, 19, 20, 21, 22, 23, 28, 29, 30
May	1, 2, 3, 4, 5, 7, 8, 9, 10, 11, 12, 13, 15, 16, 17, 18, 25, 26 27, 28, 29, 30
June	4, 5, 11, 12, 14, 15, 16, 24, 25
July	1, 2, 3, 8, 9, 12, 13, 14, 21, 22, 28, 29, 30
August	1, 2, 5, 6, 17, 18, 19, 25, 26
September	1, 2, 6, 7, 14, 15, 21, 22, 23, 24, 28, 29, 30
October	3, 4, 11, 12, 18, 19, 20, 25, 26, 27, 28, 29, 30
November	7, 8, 9, 14, 15, 16, 22, 23, 24, 25, 26, 27
December	5, 6, 12, 13, 19, 20, 21, 22, 23, 24, 25

Therapies, massage and self-pampering

January	6, 7, 13, 14, 15, 18, 19, 20, 21
February	2, 3, 9, 11, 14
March	1, 9, 14, 16, 17, 20, 23, 29
April	4, 5, 6, 10, 11, 12, 13, 17, 25, 26
May	2, 3, 7, 8, 9, 10, 11, 14, 15, 16, 17, 22, 23, 24, 31
June	3, 5, 12, 18, 19, 26, 27
July	4, 7, 8, 9, 10, 16, 23, 28, 29, 30, 31
August	3, 4, 5, 6, 7, 13, 20, 21, 24, 25, 26, 27, 28, 31
September	2, 17, 21, 28, 29

187

October	13, 14, 15, 18, 19, 21, 25, 26, 27, 28
November	2, 3, 9, 11, 14, 15, 16, 17, 21, 24, 29
December	7, 12, 13, 14, 15, 18, 19, 20, 22, 26, 27, 28, 29

ROMANCE

Pure romance, pure emotion

Two 2-in-1 anthologies each month

Available on the first Friday of every month
from WHSmith, ASDA, Tesco, Eason
and all good bookshops
Also available as eBooks
www.millsandboon.co.uk